TRACKING THE SERPENT

JOURNEYS TO FOUR CONTINENTS

JANINE POMMY VEGA

City Lights Books
San Francisco

Cover design: Rex Ray
Book design: Nancy J. Peters
Typography: Harvest Graphics

Grateful acknowledgment for the use of lines by Juan Ramón Jiménez from "Winter Scene" and "Mares," in *Lorca and Jiménez, Selected Poems,* Beacon Press, 1973. The final word in Robert Bly's translation of "Mares," changed by JPV; and from César Vallejo's "Piedra Negra Sobre Una Piedra Blanca" in *Trilce.* Lima, Peru, 1922. [Transl. by JPV].

The chapter Threading the Maze was originally published as a chapbook by Cloud Mountain Press. Sections of Atalaya appeared in *Hudson Valley Literary Supplement* and in *Unbearables* (Autonomedia.) A portion of Seeds of Travel was published in *Women of the Beat Generation* (Conari Press.)

Cataloging-in-Publication Data:

Pommy Vega, Janine.
    Tracking the serpent : journeys to four continents / by Janine Pommy Vega.
        p.   cm.
    ISBN 0-87286-327-1 (pbk.)
    1. Pommy Vega, Janine — Journeys.   2. Voyages and travels.
3. Sacred space. I. Title.
G456.R656   1997
910.4 — dc21   97-4109
                                                                CIP

City Lights Books are available to bookstores through our primary distributor: Subterranean Company, P.O. Box 160, 265 S. 5th St., Monroe, OR 97456. 541-847-5274. Toll-free orders 800-274-7826. FAX 541-847-6018. Our books are also available through library jobbers and regional distributors. For personal orders and catalogs, please write to City Lights Books, 261 Columbus Avenue, San Francisco, CA 94133.

CITY LIGHTS BOOKS are edited by Lawrence Ferlinghetti and Nancy J. Peters and published at the City Lights Bookstore, 261 Columbus Avenue, San Francisco, CA 94133.

Acknowledgments

Since its inception to its final draft, this book could not have come into being without the help of the following people:

Bill Pommy and Irene Setaro, for combing through our childhood with me.

Bob & Susan Arnold, Mikhail Horowitz, Alan Drake, Tim Knab, Hettie Jones, Peter Coyote, Ilka Scobie, Eric Hansen, Ed Levy, Ira Cohen, Peter Shotwell, Don Kennison, Guillermo Contreras, Joe Trusso, Christina Stack, Laura Kaplan, Donna Boundy, Bill Bathurst, Susan Schulman, Dave Simon, Dee Gainer, Lenka Studnickova, Harris Breiman, Betty MacDonald, Bill Hurst, Peter Hurst, Fanny Prizant, and Marilyn Allen for input, editing, reading through the various incarnations, for their enthusiasm and support.

The matchless friends and guides on the road: Yakajung Thapa, Glicerio Hinostroza, Fortunato Alvarado, Daniel Pinto Rey, Helen Anderson, Elaine Ray, Alex Braun, Laurent Braun, Billy Velarde, and Ricardo Bustamante.

Lastly, Nancy J. Peters, a great editor.

for Bob, Susan & Carson Arnold
and all fellow travelers

Contents

Seeds of Travel

Forty-seventh Street, Union City, New Jersey, across the Hudson River from Manhattan, was a working-class neighborhood of tenements and three story houses, punctuated by a few valiant trees. My elementary school was around the corner, my best friend lived across the street, and my library was three blocks away. For my first nine years, life happened in an area of about ten square blocks.

My father had a milk route from three in the morning until noon, then worked as a carpenter. Most of his time at home was spent sound asleep, while my mother, sister, brother, and I came and went around him. When I was nine he invited me to come with him on his route. I would deliver to all the walk-up apartments, and get paid a penny a bottle.

It was a Saturday in winter. We both had on watch caps to protect us against the cold. Pulling out in pitch darkness with the old truck rattling its load of empty bottles, we picked up the milk at a depot in Secaucus and made our first deliveries on the marsh lands bordering the Hackensack River. The light had been growing in the sky for some time when we turned up the grade to Hudson Boulevard. The old black truck labored noisily in the frigid shadow of the hill. The world was still sleeping. I had never been out before when no one was around.

We reached the top, by Grove Church on the corner, and swung around onto 49th Street. The sun was coming up right in our eyes. After hours of frozen darkness, the red gold light streaming down the street and flooding the inside of our truck was like a miracle. My father smiled and put down the visor. I was so struck by the beauty I couldn't speak.

Two years later on a Saturday in fall he took me on another route. Toward mid-morning we passed a little house in some tree filled neighborhood, where an old lady stood in the sun in her front yard with a rake in her hands. She was watching her cocker spaniel roll and cavort in the piles of red and yellow leaves. Inhabiting a space so unlike my own, she could have stepped out of a fairy tale about an ancient happy woman. She looked so present and alive.

Thinking of it years later, I asked my father who she was. He could not recall the woman. I described the street and the house in detail, and placed it between deliveries on our route. He said no such place existed. Whether it did or didn't doesn't matter. All I knew was I had seen something that sang inside me. And just like the sunrise, it intimated that there was a wider, more thrilling and profound reality outside the bounds of my ordinary life.

The seeds of travel, of reaching beyond familiar limits were planted there. I would step out into the unknown again and again—out of curiosity, for adventure, as a pilgrimage to find something that mattered—and each journey would show me aspects of a power I learned to accept as my own.

In high school I found Barbara, a friend who was different from the other kids: she was willing to take a risk. She looked like a showgirl; it was what she wanted to be. She wore eye makeup and had a sophisticated air. We took dance classes together. I had been reading Jack Kerouac's *On The Road*. All the characters seemed to move with an intensity that was missing in my life. A magazine article about the Beats mentioned the Cedar Bar in New York City. We decided to check it out.

Inside the smoky bar, we met by chance Gregory Corso, who seemed very interested in Barbara. Through him we met Peter

Orlovsky and Allen Ginsberg. Barbara and I began coming more often to New York. We met Herbert Huncke, Jack Kerouac, and other writers. Barbara quit school and moved in with an actor; I got a job on weekends in a coffee shop. My writing broke away from e.e. cummings imitations to my own visions and experiments with words. The bohemian life style of readings, museums, parties and intellectual discussions seemed exactly what I wanted for myself.

When I graduated from high school, I made a deal with my mother. She wanted to throw a party to celebrate my being named valedictorian. I was still underage, as she was fond of reminding me, and we had been fighting bitterly over my freedom. I agreed to the party on the condition that when it was over I could leave and she would never ask me again where I was going. I loved her and my father, I said, but I had to be about my life. She agreed to the deal.

I left for the city that night. I got a day job in an office near Bryant Park and moved in with Elise Cowen, a friend of Ginsberg's. All that winter and into the spring I read. Emily Dickinson, Christopher Smart, D.H. Lawrence, Gertrude Stein, Charles Dickens, William Blake, Catullus, John Weiners: anything anyone else was reading. This was my education.

One day in the walk-up apartment of a friend, I met Fernando Vega. I thought he might be a member of the rebel Cuban army, because of his Spanish accent, and his long dark curly hair. In fact, he was a Peruvian Jew who had recently grown earlocks as a sign of his return to his faith. He was also, I learned later, a wonderful painter. All I saw was his face and his eyes. I wrote him a poem in my high school Spanish, about Kandinsky's horse running down a mountain, and left it for him on the bathroom wall. At that time I was thin, dressed in baggy men's clothes, and wore my hair in a watch cap. My friend told me later that Fernando had thought I was a boy.

It was almost a year before I ran into him again. I'd lost my apartment, and needed a place to sleep. He invited me to his studio, showed me the single bed, then lay down in it with me. He was an exciting lover, full of intensity and sweet Latin endearments. Afterwards, he got up and disappeared. A half hour later I found him painting in the next room. I felt totally insulted. I had my clothes on and was out the door before he could speak.

Weeks later, we met again and he invited me to go back with him to see his paintings. He told me he'd been a painter all his life. Around us in the studio were abstract oil paintings—black and brown figures that seemed to swirl and move. He said his work was just beginning to gain some recognition. He'd been invited to participate in a show in the Collector's Gallery at the MOMA; the list of collectors who bought his work was growing. He was ten years older than I, and advised me to put my writing first. He said I had to be mother to the talent I'd been given.

We were both, in unconventional ways, religious. I was a renegade Christian who didn't go to church but believed in Christ and the existence of angels. He was half Jewish, half Christian by birth, but had taken on the tenets of Judaism, about which he spoke with authority. He was adamant about Jehovah being the god of everything. I figured we believed in the same thing with different names.

He had the uncanny ability to make one *see* what he was seeing. He could somehow create a vision with his hands and eyes so that I witnessed it myself. On a park bench one night, on the Fifth Avenue side of Central Park, he showed me the moment Adam and Eve were cast out of the Garden of Eden. The angel with the flaming sword was at the gate barring re-entry. Fernando said we had to walk backward through this experience to a state of simplicity, to gain the garden again. His face and eyes were shining as he spoke; in fact, he looked like Christ.

One night during a summer storm we saw a bolt of lightning, and Fernando said when lightning strikes, a man speaks about lightning. When lightning strikes as a man is speaking, it strikes the man. If it strikes after a man has spoken, it confirms what he has said. Just then lightning struck. Fernando went on speaking. After everything he said lightning struck, as though punctuating his speech. Every time it happened we looked at each other. We were both grinning and soaking wet. He asked me to move in with him.

After six months together, he asked if I would like to go to Israel with him. I said yes. Since he had overstayed his visa by two years, the only way he could leave the U.S. was by deportation. He turned himself in to Immigration authorities and was held in custody until departure. I packed for the two of us and called my mother. It was Christmas Eve; she was making yeast cake. I asked her to sit down and told her I was leaving for Israel. I asked her if they could come down and see us off. I could hear the hesitation in her voice: she was working with rising dough. She said they would try.

When I found Fernando, he was standing in the main salon of the boat with two customs agents—and my entire family. I was so touched. One by one, they all kissed me goodbye and shook hands with Fernando, whom they hardly knew. The boat pulled out. In front of us was wide, dark ocean. I could hear singing in the synagogue below. They were celebrating Chanukah. The next morning, I went up to the top deck before anyone was about. There was no land visible anywhere— no shores or boundaries. Only sun, clouds, and limitless sea.

After ten days we arrived in Israel. Fernando's sister Aurora, who lived in Jerusalem, helped us get a small room on the outskirts of town. Fernando seemed to have the traveler's knack of entering a country as though getting up to answer the door. He struck a deal with a prominent gallery in Jerusalem for advance money against the expected sales from a one-man show. In a short while we had an Arab-style house in Abu Tor, next to the barbed wire that marked the border. He began a series of large pastel drawings with swirling vivid colors. I worked for hours on poems.

Jerusalem was a walker's paradise; the view from every high place was an expanse of hills. But encircled as it was by borders and enemies, eventually one walked to all the limits and yearned to cross over. Near our house I discovered an abandoned cemetery enclosed by a stone wall, right on the border. The ten foot high gate opened onto no man's land. The rusty unused doors creaked on their hinges.

Inside, over one of the headstones, was a nearly dead tree with one bottom branch still alive. On it were yellow leaves that stood poised in the foreground like butterflies. The bare branches forked out into the clearest of blue skies. When I was fed up with words I would go there with paper, pastels, and drawing board to try to paint that tree.

One day I got up from the drawing and opened the cemetery gate. Fields, reputed to be studded with land mines, stretched before me down into the Valley of Hinnom, in Jordan. I wondered how far I would get, and stepped off the door sill. An Arab soldier on the rooftop opposite cocked his rifle. Not very far.

Looking over the rock wall by our house in the evening, I could vaguely make out the Mountains of Moab beyond the Dead Sea in the setting sun. Curiously, some evenings I could not see them at all. After weeks of watching, I made up a story about a bell ringer in his tower who discovers glorious mountains at dawn that disappear when the sun comes up. He yearns to know if they are real or not. When an angel tells him they are an entrance to heaven, it mirrored exactly how I felt about the mountains out my window I could never reach.

Our sex life was most inspired on *shabbos,* the Jewish sabbath. Everything in Jerusalem was closed; I'd cooked all the food the day before. There was nowhere to go and nothing to do but make love, eat, and walk around. We spent hours in bed, or in the large recessed window seat, or standing up in the studio, making love from every angle and position. On other days Fernando was consumed with his work, full of himself, with a somewhat patriarchal attitude toward me. I responded by burying myself in my latest poem, or reading. That our marriage survived two headstrong egos in one house was thanks to those *shabboses.*

I almost left him and returned to the States, but decided instead to leave with him for Paris. There, I sold the New York Times, worked with a folksinger—busking the movie queues while he sang—and studied French. *Clochards,* the debonnaire tramps on my rounds, taught me the argot of the street. In the mornings, I posed for art classes in L'Ecole des Beaux Arts. I tried to take seated poses so I could decipher the work of Rimbaud and Apollinaire.

Fernando and I lived on a shoestring, on the edge. Our separations grew longer, our reuniting more intense. We moved from hotel to hotel, until he made a good sale and we got our own apartment in the tenth *arrondissement,* by the Porte San Denis. He was invited to show two paintings in the Musee de L'Homme, and I gave my first reading in a small church on the Left Bank.

He introduced me to friends as, "my wife, the poet." At home, if he was painting, I would bring tea and food to his studio and leave him alone until he wanted an opinion. If I was working in my spot on the kitchen table, he did the same for me. Late at night, we walked together through the streets around the Canal St. Jacques.

The prevalence of drugs in our lives increased. One day I came in to Fernando crouching like a coiled spring in the corner. When I asked what had happened, he said he'd just taken fifty doses of mescaline. He said he had to release a killer. I told him I'd see him later. He pulled me back into the room, prying my fingers loose from the door jamb. I told him if he took my freedom, he took my life; I threatened to jump from the window. He told me to go ahead. I looked down at our concierge peering up at me. Nothing would have pleased her more than a tragedy. I wouldn't give her the satisfaction of dropping even a comb on her head.

Fernando began to go wild, throwing objects, smashing the glass on his paintings, destroying the things he had created himself. Eventually the police came. Fernando was foaming at the mouth, screaming, "I love you, I love you!" They took him to the dungeons on Ile de La Cité and asked me how many epileptic seizures he had had before. I lied and said several.

He was sent to a madhouse outside Paris. The authorities had the power to keep him there six months or longer if they chose. He pocketed the drugs they gave to sedate him, and began a series of pencil drawings of the other inmates. He was returning to himself. When I came to visit, we walked to a secluded area on the grounds, and made love in the leaves. After two months, the Peruvian consulate helped get him released.

By a stroke of good fortune, we met a woman who traded her house in Ibiza for our apartment, for a month. We left Paris almost immediately. Returning to a simpler life, we walked around, ate cheaply and very well. Fernando started a series of seascapes in oil. I met Thomas McGrath, the wonderful West Coast poet, who liked my work and made suggestions. I gave a reading in a café in the Old City. When the month was up, I volunteered to go back to sell a painting to pay the rent.

In Paris nothing went right. The collector's mother was dying; he could not be reached. My friends had no money to lend me. Two artists I posed for were out of town. Weeks passed. One night I dreamed Fernando was looking at me out of one of his paintings, as if from a mirror. Suddenly I was walking down a block in Union City, looking for him; I turned a corner and was in Paris, then Ibiza. I sat down in a cafe and felt him sitting with me at the same table, but I could not see him.

In the morning a telegram came: "Fernando is dead." I didn't believe it. In two days, another telegram: "Fernando is buried." I was trapped in the apartment, and could not move. A friend gave me the money I needed to go to Ibiza and see for myself. It was true, he was dead. I couldn't believe it. My friend, lover, and teacher was gone. The companion I addressed was not present. At twenty-three, I was a widow.

Back in New York, I lived in a small apartment. The walls were covered with Fernando's paintings; I was tearing out my heart every time I turned around. I sublet the place and left for California. In San Francisco my first book, *Poems to Fernando,* was published by City Lights, and I gave readings around the Bay Area. This was right after the Human Be-In in 1967. There were poetry readings everywhere. I began reading with the Diggers on the steps of San Francisco City Hall. Someone sent me two round-trip tickets to Maui, and I invited the poet Lenore Kandel to go with me.

I had never lived outside of cities, so close to nature. Near a little town called Haiku I moved onto the porch of a ramshackle cabin occupied by three young men. They seemed to have their own reasons for ducking out on civilization—the draft, a broken love affair, an escape from drugs—and were easy to live with. Fifty yards of baked earth and wild guava bushes stretched from my porch to the stream downhill, protected by a canopy of trees. Here was the source of the water we boiled and drank each day. The glaucous shadowy hallway provided relief from the tropical sun, and was the one absolutely private place to sit and think.

I had never lived by a stream before. The smell of the mud and wet vegetation and the constant trickling of water became like the welcome of home. I learned how to cry into the stream and let the grief go. I read the moving colors on the surface of the water at different hours, in different weathers. I became a connoisseur of dappled light. I bathed several times a day, standing knee deep in the current, and poured pailfuls of water down my back and over my head. It made me whole.

When I had to return to the mainland, I went about saying goodbye to the places I'd grown to love: the cliffs, the banana patch, the sea at sunset. The hardest to leave was the stream. In its neutral benediction, it had become a mirror of change, a mirror I would have to provide on my own. In a way I was saying goodbye to a part of myself.

My sense of pilgrimage began there—to arrive open to a place, and let its energy seep through and inform my being. That's what I'd wanted in Jerusalem with the Mountains of Moab. If a certain place is calling, let's go there! In subsequent journeys, when I looked for healing among the neolithic worship spots of Europe, or immersed myself in the teeming growth of the Amazon basin, or crossed the Andes and the Himalayas, it was with that desire: to let my personal history be overtaken by a present that was conscious of itself and infinitely alive. That consciousness I call the Mother or serpent power or Goddess has as many names as there are for God, and it doesn't matter which one we use.

The source of power resides in the interstices between one world and another, between the known and the unknown, between who we are and who we are becoming. It is our willingness to put an ear to the ground that brings the trembling of horses from a far distance. We become like the moving water, taking the river bed with us as we go. The universe loves devoted travelers. We are her witnesses.

Years later, I was climbing in the Andes with Laurent, Fernando's brother Alex's son. We'd come up from sea level to 11,000 feet two days before, and had driven that morning up to 13,000 feet, where we'd left the car. We were making for Lake Churup at 15,000 feet, by the foot of the Churup glacier in Peru's highest range. Friends who'd come with us fell behind and soon it was just the three of us—my nephew, the guide, and me. It was early afternoon when we arrived at the small waterfall, patch of green grass, and red scrabbly *quenhual* trees clutching the rock face. They made an oasis to the eye after the dry windswept terrain.

We made our way hand over hand up the rock face, and scaled a series of ledges to reach the top. Down the other side was the bluest quietest lake I'd ever seen. The turquoise water reflected the massive glacier and granite wall above it with barely a ripple. Lake Churup.

The sun was blazing down. My nephew and the guide stretched out on the rock to take a snooze under their caps. I stepped away from them, down to the lake, in search of more shade. A leafy *quenhual* branch made a small pool of shadow on the stones at the water's edge. I squatted in it, hugging my knees, and lost myself to the immensity of the silence, and the brightness of the glacier in the sun. Suddenly there was a barely perceptible change in air pressure around my shoulders, and the slightest whirring sound. I looked up in time to catch a wild duck flying over. He disappeared behind the granite wall, and I sat stunned as the intensity of silence returned.

The stillness had been so vast and complete, a few feathers moving had been enough to break it. The silence had a palpable presence that swallowed all thought. Any barriers I had slipped off like masks. There was no *me* left.

When I returned to the boys on the rock, I recounted this immense event— a duck passed over— and the guide nodded. He was smoking a cigarette. He patted the rock we all sat on with the flat of his hand.

"This is life, right here," he said. He waved his hand toward the long slopes, going down to the valley, and from there to the towns, far below. "The rest— all of that— is just stories."

My desire to slip away from the stories and the choices we make to secure our identity in everyday life has borne fruit again and again. To go on a pilgrimage, I discovered, you do not need to know what you are looking for, only that you are looking for *something,* and need urgently to find it. It is the urgency that does the work, a readiness to receive that finds the answers.

Threading the Maze

Driving to work in early May, 1982, I was in a head-on collision. It was an overcast morning, and a car was coming at me in my lane of the two lane highway—Route 55 in upstate New York. I realized as it barreled toward me that the car was not passing anyone. I had two choices: swerve to the right into the ditch and perhaps overturn, or take the other lane. I chose the left lane; at the very last second the other car did, too. No body should ever have to know such violence.

My head went through the windshield, and I was lucky—the rims of my sunglasses were so thick they saved my eyes. At the moment of impact I shouted out and bit through my tongue. I staggered out of my car—moving toward the other car to help the driver, then moving away in case the cars blew up.

Someone said, "For heaven's sake, lie down!"

In the weeks that followed, as I convalesced, I read *The Silbury Treasure* and *The Great Goddess Rediscovered* by Michael Dames. Dames said Silbury, located in Marlboro County in the south of England, was the tallest prehistoric structure in Europe. It was neither a monument to a king nor the burial place of a warrior, as the experts claimed, but a huge man-made hill built to represent the womb of the Goddess. The moat around it, filled with water, was her body reflecting the sky.

On Lammas (from "loaf mass"), a festival day of wheat harvest that falls around August eighth, the moon rising over the moat and reflected in the water portrayed the baby coming out of the hill and being born. The ancient people, working in synchronicity with the Goddess at this moment of birth, went down then to their own fields to cut down the new grain.

As I read into the early morning hours, night after night, an owl began calling at my window. Slowly the idea coalesced of making a pilgrimage to the ancient sites where the Goddess had been worshiped: Silbury, Glastonbury, Avebury, the high hills of Ireland, and Chartres Cathedral in France. I needed a power and protection in myself. I needed to reaffirm something in me that felt ripped apart and empty.

It was summer before I was strong enough to set out. I made for London, the city of all the writers I'd loved since I had started to read. I dropped my bags in the dormitory room of a cheap hotel, and ran out to find Westminster Abbey. Once inside the cathedral, however, my awe at visiting Chaucer, Tennyson and Wordsworth shifted. In the gloomy light rococo displays celebrated the winning of wars, male dominance, and the privilege of the upper classes. Many Georges slew many dragons, and every one of them was the Goddess.

The altar where coronations took place, surrounded by the seats of knights with their flashcard breastplates and tiny flags, was cut off from the main body of the church. This was not an edifice of shared worship with the common people, but a clannish affair of the ruling classes. Interred in the walls of the right side of the church were all the statesmen and politicians; only the left side held some glimmer of hope in the writers and poets. But even Chaucer, who'd been the first writer buried, had been chosen not for his work but because he'd had a sinecure in the church. After hours of plaques and the history of kings, I burst out into the wind off the Thames and realized I'd been holding my breath.

In the rainy and drizzly days that followed, I visited Virginia Woolf's Bloomsbury, and Charles Dickens' house, with his wonderful dark wooden desk. I saw the ruins of a church where Charles Lamb had studied; I met a woman in the Victoria Station Tea Room whose father had known A.E. and Yeats. I sold some of my books to The Poetry Society, but my spirits under the wet sky were beginning to flag.

One afternoon, as I turned toward my lodgings, a stiff wind moving the cloud cover across the sky made me want to hike out into the open. Soon a street sign said I'd reached the Great West Road. I kept on going. As I crossed a bridge, the first sun in days shot through and widened out to a gold and crimson sunset dead ahead. It was time to leave London for the west.

The Tourist Directory gave me a list of bed & breakfasts in Glastonbury, Somerset County, on the southwest coast of England. I landed a room at Mrs. Kinsman's, whose lodgings, she said, were a mile from the center of town, but very comfortable. I had time for one last stop.

At the British Museum I went directly to the Neolithic corner. There were the antler picks and stone implements. There were the pictures of prehistoric buildings with the round rooms and round alcoves in the form of the Goddess, and scientific pamphlets singularly uncommitted as to her worship. I could have been a Jew looking at the ancient Torah in the synagogue of the oldest quarter, where the Baal Shem Tov once lived, in Prague. There was the squatting Goddess, the owl-eyed Goddess, the antler mask! I felt like jumping up and down.

My first glimpse of the Glastonbury tor, about twelve miles distant, was from the bus window. It looked like one of the square pillars on the Moon card of the Tarot deck, an image disconcerting in its familiarity. If it's so, as Jung says, that there are certain universal glyphs imprinted on the human psyche, then this tor was one of them. Legends say the earliest Christian monks perceived the fire energy emanating from the hill and built a church on top of it dedicated to Michael, the archangel of fire, to govern the primordial powers. But an earthquake toppled the church and all that remained was the pagan symbol of a lone tower on a hill.

We were coming down Route 39 from Bath. I was dozing in

my seat when a car passed by with the license plate, O★W★L. I looked up with a start. The tor stood gray and old in the distance, then hid behind an intervening hill. I believe a pilgrimage relies on signposts, outside images or events that strike a chord with the personal storehouse in one's psyche. How else explain my sudden sense of well-being?

Mrs. Kinsman's gentleman friend Earl met me at the bus stop and brought me to her bed & breakfast. The one mile distance from the center of town went uphill toward the tor. Mrs. Kinsman, a chipper woman in her late fifties with straight dark hair pulled over her ears, welcomed me warmly. She took me upstairs and stood at the door as I dropped my bags and went to the window. It faced the tor itself, about a half mile up the hill.

"People come here for a lot of reasons," she said. "One woman spent the night in that bed, and came down the next day, demanding another room. She said the tower had invaded her dreams, and she could not sleep."

"I wouldn't have minded those dreams, myself," I said.

"Did you know there's a line starting from Michael's Mount, in the southwest corner of Britain, in Land's End, that comes right through here, then passes through Avebury and Silbury as well? You should look at it on a map. A straight line. Quite remarkable." She handed me the key.

Situated in southwest England, Glastonbury is set in a lowland several miles in from the sea. At high tide the sea is kept back by the dikes at Bridgewater Bay, but the fog rolls in from time to time, and covers the fields and pastures like a sea itself.

Legend says Joseph of Arimathaea was directed to take the grail or chalice containing Jesus' sweat and blood, and go northward along the coast until his ship came to an inland sea with three round hills. He did so and arrived at Glastonbury. On Wearyall Hill, the first hill he came to, he leaned on his Levantine thorn tree staff, and it burst into bloom, though it was December. The Druids recognized him as a priest with a powerful sun god of his own.

Joseph hid the grail inside the deep square well on Chalice Hill, in the shadow of the third mound, five hundred feet above the tidewater sea, Tor Hill.

"To actually be sitting here, and not in the imagination!" I wrote in my journal. "I wake up from my nap to the tower over my shoulder, etched against the sky, blocking out the northern constellations."

I went down the hill to explore Glastonbury. Halfway to town I realized I wasn't interested in milling around with the tourists in the town square, so I doubled back to a pub I'd passed, The Green Swordsman. A wave of heat hit me at the door. The pub was packed with local townspeople celebrating the weekend or the middle of summer. They seemed to touch one another more than in American bars. It reminded me of animals grouping up in a field—a celebration of elbows, shoulders, buttocks, breasts—while each person maintained the stand-up posture of holding a drink and talking.

I met two men standing together; both were called Colin. When I said I was a poet, they asked me to recite something.

> There was an old lady
> Lived under the hill.
> And if she's not gone
> She lives there still.

was all I could think of. We laughed together as though it were immensely funny.

Walking back to my room after closing time, I took a circuitous route along the High Way, and looked at the tor in the moonlight. A herd of placid cows grazing on the lowest skirts of the hill looked curiously in my direction. I realized there was no need to go downhill and cross Chalice Hill as the map indicated. I could go straight up.

The next day I climbed from behind Mrs. Kinsman's. The tor was a four-sided gray stone tower, hollow inside like a chimney stack, with the clouds scudding across the opening at the top.

There were no windows. According to tradition, before the church and tower were built, the hill had held a circle of stones where the god of fire had been worshipped. West was the direction for fire in the old religion. The western face of the tower was the only one carved in bas-relief; it depicted a scale on the right, and a woman and milk cow on the left of the entrance.

Around the tor was undulating pasture land, ending on three sides at a line of hills. In the distant past the ancient people had built earthworks to mirror the prominent constellations in the northern sky, and through the years they had gotten incorporated into the landscape of Somerset County. Map in hand, I stood imagining the giant figures stretched out over the earth and defined by roads, stone walls, and bridges; but without a compass my placement of the effigies was pure conjecture. Groups of hikers—in twos and threes, by the dozen, in families—came and went. They gave the hill a tramped-down feeling.

Descending the western face of Tor Hill, I entered the Chalice Well garden. I made my way past terraces of flowers to a large square wading pool fed by the water gushing from a lion's head in the stone wall. I tried the water, filled my flask, then climbed to the well. The metal lid was a design of intersecting circles, forming a fish between them. I lifted the lid. The well shaft was about nine feet deep, and large enough for several people to stand in. On the far side of the stone sill was another chamber under the ground.

The water was a rusty red; the rocks in the well shaft were stained carnelian. I closed the lid and noticed the petrified snails imbedded in the rocks at my feet. The garden seemed so lovingly tended. The only sound was the gurgling of water beneath the lid. The feeling of peace was enormous. I suddenly realized that in the depths of myself was everything I needed to be healed. I wept, tracing the snails in the stones with my fingers.

It was late afternoon when I walked through a side gate toward the abbey ruins. I came to an old garden with the biggest oak trees I had ever seen. Obviously private, it could have served as the cloistered courtyard of a monastery. With the shrubbery, stone benches, and patches of flowers, it had the studied artlessness of a formal English garden. From somewhere on the far side came the sounds of a calliope.

The shadowed paths beneath the ancient oaks were dappled with red gold sun. Birds flitted about and sang in the upper branches. A monk, reading on a stone bench, looked up impassively as I walked by, and went back to his book. At the bottom of the garden an ornate gate opened onto the abbey grounds. Built in the twelfth century, "the longest church in England" was laid atop the remnants of a much older church, circa 200-300 A.D. Legend says Joseph of Arimathaea built a wattle church, around which he lived with his twelve companions in a circle of cells, next to a graveyard of pre-Christian chieftains.

I crossed the field and came to a stone pool constructed, the sign said, to keep the abbot's fish until Friday. By the ruins around me I could imagine the beehive of activity in the old days. The stone kitchen held a fireplace big enough to roast whole animals on the spit. The smokehouse preserved the fish and meat. I could imagine the mead, honey, loaves of newly baked bread, the corn and barley, the freshly killed game, the fruit and wine. Since everyone had to send in their tithes to the abbey barns, the abbot, like any other prosperous lord, must have laid a sumptuous table. The abbey had been a miniature fiefdom, and the coin of the realm belief.

I woke before dawn to a sea of mist below my window. The trees behind Mrs. Kinsman's house were half buried in white. Only the tor stood out on its hill, until the mist swirled in and swallowed everything. I thought it would be a splendid opportunity to watch the clouds cover the world from the isolation of the tower. Then I fell back asleep.

By the time I awoke, the mist had burned off and Mrs. Kinsman, dressed in a large white apron, was bustling about the kitchen. She and Earl had gone blackberry picking the day before;

she was preparing to make preserves. Along with toast and jam, she'd laid out yogurt and berries for me. Much of the food she served came from her own garden. She dried herbs for tea, made soups from leeks, nettles, and other wild greens, and in the midst of a small town kept a country kitchen.

She rolled up her sleeves. "With a sharp look-out, there's no reason you can't eat all year from what grows right around here."

Earl boiled the jars while she prepared berries. They worked well together. From the moment I had declared myself a vegetarian, she'd served up one wonderful meal after another: scalloped potatoes, vegetable casseroles, salads of wild greens, stewed fruits. She had a generator to run her freezer and pump, should the electricity go out, and seemed to manifest in her bed & breakfast the concept that self-sufficiency was not only possible but necessary. Hard work was the only substitute for waste. She used no paper towels.

After breakfast I climbed straight up Tor Hill in the sun. Reaching the northern wall of the tower, I looked out at the countryside. A farmer was haying his field directly below. Instead of going at it methodically from one side to the other, back and forth, until he'd cut the whole field, he started in the middle of one side and covered the whole perimeter first. Then he doubled back along the first swath until he came to the starting point, and doubled back again. By doubling back along the inside track, he was leaving a trail of concentric circles intersected by the corridor in from the starting place, which remained unmowed. I had never seen a field cut that way. The pattern reminded me of something I couldn't put my finger on. I watched him for quite a while before I had it. It looked like a maze.

I had been reading about how the primordial people in their earthworks had portrayed earth energy as a snake coiled in concentric circles. They had banked each mound into a spiral: a dragon circling and squeezing the hill. Starting from the cow pasture, Tor Hill was graded three times around in a processional ascent to the top. The work was then to ascend the spiral, to thread the maze.

It was a brilliantly clear day. The man worked slowly in the hot sun. I saw that when he arrived at the center, he would cut down the last corridor on his way out to where he'd started. He could not reach the center without mowing the whole field, and when he finished, he would have created a wonderful labyrinth defined by the fallen grasses. Threading the maze meant snaking your way through the passageways of a wide expanse before reaching the core. It meant touching down and covering every inch of it, over and over in diminishing circles until you reached the heart.

It was my last day in Glastonbury. I left in a steady rain and took the processional ascent up Tor Hill. The cows were dripping as they grazed in the pasture. Circling the hill as I climbed, I could see the different places I'd walked: Wearyall Hill with the thorn trees, the road towards Bath, the bookstores in town. The landscape was made to order for a walker, and I could walk three hours easily now before I had to lie down.

Chalice Hill was perfectly round beneath me. Mrs. Kinsman had said that most of the hills in Somerset County were graded with a path spiralling to the top. I looked around. The countryside was dotted with hills, dragons sitting on their haunches in the rain.

At the top, I stood at the tower entrance with a compass and a map of the giant star effigies. To my surprise, the tower was not lined up exactly north east south west, but twenty-seven degrees off, counterclockwise. What I had taken for Castle Cary, nine miles to the east, was something else. People kept streaming up and down the hill, some with umbrellas, some without, while I studied the map. A sudden quiet made me look up. There was no one around me. I circled the tor. No one.

I jumped inside the tower, and did what I'd been wanting to do since my first visit. I sang out one note loud and clear. It reverberated up the flue like it was coming from the entrails of the hill. The acoustics were wonderful. I imagined the sound as a pillar of fire, going up the chimney and out the top— not burning fire exactly, but a flame with the nighttime colors of the northern lights. I was imagining how it would look in the distance, a steady glow with a slight flickering at the edges, when two boys burst through the entry.

They were about seven, both soaking wet. They seemed to have escaped someone's jurisdiction and were making the most of it, chasing each other around the tor with the boundless energy of puppies. They shouted names up the tower shaft, and hearing the echo, called out like Tarzan and hurled themselves beneath the iron bar at the entrance into the mud. An angry voice was coming closer. I thought I'd make my escape. I hated to see all that energy subdued.

I walked down toward Chalice Hill in a driving wind. The rain subsided, and flowers in the garden stood out in the silver light—snapdragons, roses, marigolds, delphinium, dahlias, zinnias, cosmos—a wild array of colors. The sun pushed suddenly through the clouds. Tor Hill was still in the rain, but the sun lit up the garden. Over the lower shoulder of the hill between the tower and the well was a rainbow.

Journal entry:

> Thank you for the peace here,
> It is the whole animal that worships,
> not the soul and body splintered.
> Until I know that, I will carry you inside
> until I am you.

Leaving, I noticed the rose-covered gate I had left ajar was closed—a generous gesture on the gardener's part. While I'd sat there no one had entered. I filled my flask at the well. I had an hour before the bus left for Marlborough, the closest town to Silbury Hill.

Through the dreary afternoon we drove due east into the rain along highway A-4. A faulty exhaust circulated carbon monoxide back into the bus, so I opened a window. I was half asleep, staring vaguely off to the right, when we passed a white horse carved into the chalk cliff above the road—a beautiful stylized running horse, like the ones I'd seen in the earliest weavings of Tarabuco, Bolivia.

I rummaged through my bag for my journal, and found myself straining forward in my seat, like a bird dog in the presence of game. We went around a bend. Thirty yards from the road was an unusually symmetrical but otherwise ordinary cone shaped hill thrust up from the valley floor. Silbury. The hill built by the ancient people to portray the Goddess as pregnant mother, the giver of grain.

Constructed nearly five thousand years ago with amazing meticulousness, Silbury Hill was widely believed to be the burial mound of a great king. John Aubrey, a writer in the 1600s, told King Charles II that "tradition had it King Sil or Zel was buried inside the mound on horseback, and that the hill was raised while a posset of milk was seething." A posset was a hot drink made of milk curdled with ale or wine. Subsequent centuries saw several major excavations—from the top of the hill down, and lateral tunnels in to the core—in search of King Sil.

What they found instead was dirt. A central area sixty-five feet across was enclosed by a low fence. In the middle was a three foot high mound of clay and flints, covered with eight feet of layered turf and soil, extending out to the fence. From the central core were spokes of twisted grass that radiated outward like a spider's web to the edge of the existing hill. On top of the turf were layers of chalk and gravel; atop that, seventeen foot high chalk blocks were laid within the borders of roped web. The blocks were mounted up in six tiers to the top. All the angles were filled in with rubble to achieve the roundness, and the entire surface was planted with grass. The result was a stable round hill that had not eroded in five thousand years.

What the excavating scientists found were bits of deer antler, moss that had retained its color and freshness, remnants of mistletoe and twisted string. There was no one buried, no horse, no king. The hill resembled a pregnant belly.

Six miles down the road was the town of Marlborough. I had

ten blocks to walk from the bus stop. As I started out, the rain increased. By the time I reached the Bed & Breakfast, everything was soaked through except my typewriter. The woman who greeted me at the door was an arch grandmotherly lady—the severe kind, with a storehouse of reserve—who showed me upstairs to my room.

The damp chilly room had a bed and an old wooden closet. The walls were bare except for the signs:

NO SMOKING

NO BATHS AFTER 9 P.M.

NO VISITORS PERMITTED

NO EATING IN ROOM

ALL LODGERS MUST VACATE BY 11 A.M.

The woman regarded me as I stood in the puddle growing around my feet; her smile settled like a cold pall over my shoulders. She offered no tea, no towel, nothing. She was not Mrs. Kinsman. I decided to leave my bags where they were, and look for some warmth.

It was a grim little town in the rain. Gray buildings, gray streets, not many trees. The people passing were tight-lipped, unfriendly. No smiles, no nods in my direction. My lower back was aching from the dampness. Maybe it was all the reading I'd done on Silbury, or the friendliness I'd met with in Glastonbury, but I found it amazing that people living near a worship spot so profound could be so down in the mouth.

It was August seventh. The next day would be Lammas, the midway point between summer solstice and autumn equinox, the height of summer when the ancient people had celebrated the cutting of wheat in synchronicity with the earth's labor. Wouldn't any of that old joy still live in the hearts of the people? I caught the eye of a thin woman under a black umbrella. She frowned and looked away. Then again, perhaps the ruthlessness of the church in stamping out all vestiges of the old religion had wiped out all the merriment as well.

At the Information Centre, the woman in charge said I could catch a local bus in the morning that went out along Route A-4, past Silbury.

"It *is* possible to climb the hill," she said officiously, "but unfortunately, Silbury is closed."

"How can you close a hill?" I said.

Behind me someone laughed—a young man, maybe German or Swedish, a tourist like myself.

"Next!" barked the woman.

Outside in the steady rain, dusk was closing in and my jacket was dripping. I made for the lights of a pub, The Jolly Butcher. A rush of warm air greeted me at the door. By the cheery hubbub, I gathered that any merry souls left in town were probably all gathered there.

"What'll ya have, me love?" boomed a friendly voice.

I ordered a hot tea and shook out my hair.

"Beastly day," said the barman, who introduced himself as Jeremy. "After you've taken the chill off with that—" he laid down the tea, "you'll want to try our ale." He looked at the company in the bar. "They all swear by it. Isn't that right, gents?"

Round-faced and ruddy complexioned, Jeremy looked perfectly suited for his job. Bustling about in an apron tied around his solid girth, he seemed to have a quip or comment for everyone. Rather than risk going back to the rain, I ordered some pub grub—cold cheese sandwiches and those awful hardboiled eggs in a jar—and washed it down with the local ale. It was light brown, with a slightly bitter aftertaste, and every bit as excellent as he'd said.

A bus load of senior citizens came in, fresh from having toured Avebury, the circle of giant standing stones, one mile from Silbury. After traipsing about in the rain they looked ready for some refreshments. They filed in toward the tables in the back and called out their orders before they sat down. Thirty shots of rye, each with a pint of ale on the side. Not one cup of tea. Jeremy fussed around them until they were served and settled in; then he opened the cellar door to go down for more bottles.

"No singin' whilst I'm gone now, old 'uns!" he called gaily up the cellar stairs.

In the ensuing hours I met all the local patrons; after several pints I'd told everyone of my plan for the following day. The other tourist from the Information Centre had come in and taken the stool beside me. He introduced himself as Werner. He was German and sort of good-looking, but carried himself a little stiffly for someone so young. He said he'd be going to Avebury the next morning and asked to accompany me to my hill.

I was taken aback. I'd always envisioned going alone. It hadn't occurred to me to bring anyone else, but a pilgrimage is open-ended: if I were in charge, what good would it be? I shrugged and tentatively agreed. He seemed to really want to go, and I could always leave him somewhere if he got in the way.

He offered to walk me home. On the rainy streets I told him about Silbury: how the hill was the baby and the moat around it, filled with water reflecting the sky, was the mother. How the people waited in the night for the moon to rise over the hill and shine in the water: the reflection represented the baby coming out from the vulva of the hill. But the baby needed water from the well and milk from the breast, and the people waited until dawn, when the sun lit up the mother's breast, and the baby had food to eat. Then they went to their fields to harvest their grain in synchronicity with the earth, and didn't sleep until it was all cut down.

Werner nodded at intervals. I couldn't tell what he thought. We agreed to meet at nine at the bus stop. It was just after midnight when we reached my lodgings, which were locked. I knocked and waited. As he turned to go, an owl called from up the road. The old woman appeared at the door, and I nodded pleasantly.

"I'm sorry I'm late."

"Well, I guess you are!" she sniffed, and turned on her heel.

It was hard to believe the morning belonged to the same climate as the night before; the hot sultry air felt like it had come from the Mato Grosso in Brazil. In my pack I had a flask of water from Chalice Well, my notebook and pen, and two cheese sandwiches Jeremy had wrapped for me the night before. Down the street I could see Werner with a pack of his own. He bowed slightly as I came running up, and the bus pulled in.

Six miles outside of town the driver left us off at the causeway that connected the highway and the hill. Crossing over, we ignored the signs.

CLOSED!

NO TRESPASSING!

We scaled the fence and started up. The moat around the hill was filled with silt and wild grass, but it was easy to imagine it full of water. From the top we picked out the mammoth longitudinal profile of the mother, squatting in labor. Her head and neck stretched toward the west; her back faced north, her thigh to the east; coming around to the front, her knee faced south. Then came the causeway we'd crossed, and the inter-causeway moat, where the baby would come out of her vulva when the moon shone in the water.

The other causeway underlined her breast, also facing south. The outline of her whole body relied on those two causeways, over her knee and under her breast. Without them she would have been just a round amorphous pond, without proportion. I could see how the moon as it rose would travel up the inter-causeway moat to become the baby on its mother's knee. But even without the drama of a moon, the magnitude of the hill, when you considered it was dug out and heaped up by hand, was staggering.

At the top of the hill the observation platform was like a natural ledge. We spread out our things on the grass. Swallowhead Spring, visible off to the right across a small road, was the underground spring that ran only in February and March. It joined the Winterbourne River to become the river Kinnet, or as the local people called it, Cunnit, which filled the moat around Silbury Hill. Swallowhead was the cunt that gave forth life in early spring, and ran white from the chalky ground at the base of the hill, "like a seething posset of milk." The confluence of physical facts with the ancient belief system was wonderful.

The sun seemed to be ironing the landscape flat. There were no sounds, no breeze, no gnats, no cars on the road, no people walking anywhere on the wide flat landscape below. Werner and I looked at each other. As though by some prior agreement, we took off our clothes, laid them on the coarse grass, and began making love.

His face turned suddenly beautiful and alive. Sweating and moving in the sun together, I found him less experienced than I. When he came, he got angry with himself. He averted his face but I pulled him back to look at me. I was glad we had shared the closeness; I was glad it had happened as though arranged. He reached up and pulled the hair away from my forehead.

"What happened to your temple?"

"Head-on collision."

He pulled my head down and kissed it gently.

A little black and white dog jumped onto our ledge, and started yipping. We threw our clothes on just in time. A man, woman, and young girl waved as they headed for the top. I started putting my things together.

"Did you know we would do this?" he asked. "I mean, with all your talk of synchronicity?"

"No."

Shouldering my pack, I saw him watching me.

"Well, let's say once I saw the place, I thought we might."

There was an ease between us as we scrambled down the hill. We hopped the fence and crossed the flat plain toward Avebury henge. A circle of giant sarsen stones stood upright in the sun. I headed for the trees at the edge of the field. Werner wanted to see if he could find the stones with the most power by the feel of them against his body. Sitting in the shade of the ancient beeches, I watched him lean against them one by one. According to theorists, anywhere you find the Goddess celebrated in one form, you will find nearby her other aspects as well. At Silbury the Goddess was mother, in the barrows nearby she was crone or destroyer. But at Avebury she was the lover.

I looked at the things in my hands: four shiny dark green beech leaves, a chalky pyramidal stone from the Avebury circle, a handful of wild grass from Silbury Hill. Why was I gathering these things? The souvenirs I brought home were always stones, sticks, bones, and the like. I put them in a drawer of sacred objects; some disintegrated, some didn't. After a time I forgot where they came from, but it was an animal delight to hold them, and physical proof of my passage.

Journal entry: "Where does the personal leave off, and the universal begin? Am I the actor or acted upon? Thomas Merton said they'd had a thousand years of continuous peace in the Monte Alban civilization in Mexico. Each person became his or her function, and their names described what was required of them by the common belief system. In the dovetailing layers, private desire was synchronous with communal intent and a continuity of belief. Am I the mother then, or the pristess and servant? The seeker or place of worship? I am filled with magnitude and presence, the sun and wind in the circle of the horizon."

The stars wheeled over the deck as the captain brought the ferry around from due west to southwesterly. We were headed down from Liverpool to Rosselare, near Dublin. At 52 degrees latitude, Auriga, the charioteer was much higher overhead than I was used to seeing it; Capella, its brightest star, stood out among the circumpolar constellations. Next to the summer triangle I found Hercules. He was the dominant male in the Neolithic star effigies of Somerset. The name for Hercules, one of the oldest known constellations, had changed through the ages. Called simply *the kneeler* in old Arabic texts, he was depicted either kneeling or running and swinging a club.

The dominant female of the earthworks was Virgo, who held

sheaves of wheat. The second wave to migrate up from the fertile crescent were sun worshipping people who brought the plough. As they wrested the northern lands from the matriarchal tribes, the kneeler, I thought, might have taken up what became his cudgel and beaten them into submission.

Lifeboats ringed the deck. I considered slipping into one of them to sleep. There were no cabins left on board, and I'd been traveling for sixteen hours. In Dublin I would take a train to Sligo on the west coast. The Mother of Harvests had been celebrated there as late as the 1940s on what they called High Sunday in August in the high caves overlooking the countryside.

The night was extremely clear. Music blared from the disco bar as I leaned back in the deck chair. I could even see the smaller stars in the nameless kneeler, as he sprawled west of Ophiucus to Draco, the Dragon. Starting from the star in the kneeler's head, there was a figure with his right arm flung out, and his left upraised, holding a club. He was kneeling with his right foot on the dragon's head.

In the Chaldean myth he is the sun god Izhdubar, who slew the dragon Tiamat, after which he had twelve adventures that later were to become the tasks of Hercules. He slew the dragon, or was standing on her head in this image, but in an earlier age he probably did no such thing. Perhaps he knelt in a field, lifting a stake above his head to thrust it down into the earth like a plough. Perhaps he was simply kneeling. Before us the sickle moon sunk into the sea.

Travel equals suffering. After thirty-six hours by bus, boat, train, and foot, I reached the Woodbine Cottage in Rosses Point, seven miles from Sligo. I'd stayed there some years before, and was happy to find it empty.

"So you've come back to us, Yank," the owner said, when I tracked him down. He counted the money I gave him, and handed me the keys. "You can have her for a week."

I flung open the cottage windows. Ben Bulben on the right

looked like a green whale headed west under a seafaring sky. To the left was Knocknarea, with her distinctive profile; on the flat green summit was a thirty-five foot heap of stones, reputed to be Maeve's cairn. Yeats had spent his childhood summers flanked by those two mountains.

Maeve was the wild goddess of war, who led armies of her own into battle. Legend said she required the intimate company of countless kings and heroes, at least thirty lovers a day. But just as the goddess Bride, or Bridget, had been reduced to the confines of sainthood under centuries of Christian influence, Maeve had been demoted to a mortal queen. She was buried, they said, next to one of her warriors, who was standing upright. Others said he was on horseback, like King Sil. But the five thousand year old cairn had never been penetrated to make sure. Unlike the English at Silbury, the Irish were very cautious about those things.

The following morning I hitched a ride out to Knocknarea, which stood a thousand feet above Rosses Point. I located the footpath and looked about until I found a round gray rock the size of a duck egg. The cairn at the top had grown with the rock each visitor had added to the pile. I climbed past a group of men haying a field on the flanks of the mountain.

The sky had a curious silver light as though it might clear. At the summit I added my stone to the cairn. The top of Ben Bulben was clouded over. I picked out the cottage in Rosses Point and noted the fields behind it, where I'd been told a fairy fort still existed.

Suddenly the light changed. Driven by the wind, a mist swirled around the cairn. All directions and viewpoints were gone. I thought about Yeats's story of Red Hanrahan up on Ben Bulben as the mist had closed in, and the little door in the earth had opened and out streamed the fairy folk led by the Daughter of the Silver Hand. The mist raced past me, over the cairn and down the hill like a stream of figures in flowing garments.

I tried to imagine their faces. Who were they? Goddesses, gods, heroes from Ireland's history? I hugged myself to keep warm in the driving wind. The white wall in motion was dense around me; Maeve was cut off in the clouds from the world below. I circled the hilltop twice before finding the path. Three hundred feet down the fog disappeared except on the cairn above me. Perhaps Maeve had wanted the hill to herself. Perhaps the rush of figures *was* herself.

In the days that followed, I regained the pleasures of being among the Irish again: the "crack" in the pubs (not the drug, but their word for the talk), the glib retort, their way of looking at the least bit of blue in the sky, declaring it "a grand day," and launching out in walking shoes the minute it stopped raining. But I was finding myself in the late nights coming face to face with the bias against homosexuals and women. Certain turns of phrase would raise the hair on my neck, and I'd direct my furious response at the speaker's skull like a laser beam. Someone said, though it didn't look like I was having much fun, he thought I might be.

One late afternoon I entered a pub I didn't know. The woman behind the bar was like something out of Irish legends: beautiful, sexy, passionate, witty, possessive, the center of attention. How she walked, how she moved, how she put a glass down was riveting. It wasn't her appearance—she wore a baggy T-shirt and nondescript pants, and her hair hung around her face in greasy strands—it was the way she glided from place to place. Her name was Kathleen. Of the twenty people in the bar, everyone watched or was aware of her, all connected to her in some way like strands to the center of a web.

That night I returned, hoping to talk to her. Instead, an amiable man with thinning hair looked up and waved me to a stool as though he knew me. His name was Padraic, pronounced Porrick, and he was the owner. As the lone traveler, I took up my usual occupation of reading the people around me, observing details I would ordinarily not notice were I engaged in conversation. Padraic's long fingers were stained from smoking, his fingernails bitten to the quick.

The place was crowded. He was doing a brisk business. Every time he came down to my end of the bar we talked. When I mentioned I was a writer, he said he had been one too, until he had inherited the pub, which had become the sole livelihood for him and his family, and had taken away any time for writing.

"My wife works days," he said, emptying the glasses. "Between the two of us we're lucky if we get the kids fed and off to school and the place opened on time."

So the fabulous Kathleen was his wife. Two young men had just come in and were standing beside me holding hands. The taller was clearly the more delicate of the two.

"Guinness for the both of you, Tom?"

The shorter man nodded. When he left with the drinks, I noticed the pink triangle sewed onto his sleeve. It was a replica of the insignia the Nazis required all homosexuals wear in Germany during the war. I looked at Padraic.

"You've probably noticed how the people here don't take kindly to any differences," he said. "These lads have been marching the streets of Sligo with their triangles, and this is not Dublin. They've earned the right to hold hands and declare themselves," he looked around the pub, "and I'll have no man tell me otherwise."

I took his hand like a comrade at the barricades. "But what about the women?" I said. "What about Mrs. Bob Callahan, and Mrs. Jim Feeney, addressed as though they had no names of their own?"

He had deep creases at his eyes when he smiled. "I'm against it, but they're the ones'll have to stand up and change it— like Tom and Jimmy there."

The air was thick with smoke and talk. People stood two and three deep at the bar. Padraic had to dash from one end of the bar to the other to keep up. When he reached my glass again, I asked why he didn't have help.

"My wife usually works with me Saturday nights, but the kids are at her mother's. And I think—well, we have an open marriage—I think she's busy right now."

When the crowd thinned out, I was still in my corner. He pulled up a chair by the sink and sat down.

"I tried an open marriage once," I said. "It was Hell. It takes so much courage and so much trust, or it just falls apart. And sometimes it just falls apart anyway."

He took his first shot of the night. His nose in profile was aquiline above the soft sagging to his lower face.

"Kathleen has made love to every man in this town, I'll wager. She loves me and she loves the kids, but it's something she needs to do. When the kids came, there was no time for her art. She's an actress. Now with the pub there's even less, so she makes love." He faced me squarely. "It's an open marriage by default. Either open or no marriage at all."

"And what about you? Is it open at your end, too?"

He shot me a look, and smiled slightly. "Sometimes."

I have a book I'd like to lend you. It's Flann O'Brien's *The Third Policeman*. Do you know it?"

His smile grew. "I know of it, but I haven't read it."

"I have it with me. I think you'd like it."

It turned out he knew the cottage in Rosses Point.

"Perhaps I'll have someone work for me, and come out tomorrow night."

"That's a grand idea."

Woodbine was an unpretentious cottage with three small rooms and an outhouse. The last time I'd lived there I'd been finishing a book of poems. I was pleased to see the desk I'd pushed to the window had not been moved. Unlike England, there were no specific sites of pilgrimage I sought in Ireland; I didn't even know the caves where the Goddess was last worshiped. But I was open to the hints and traces of her through the culture itself.

The people always referred to Eire as female. They believed in nature spirits, the wee folk, whether they spoke of it or not. There were stags with great antlers on the stones in the oldest graveyards: this most male element in the natural world also represented the

Goddess. That morning the grocer had unrolled a frayed ordnance map of Sligo, enlarged to include every ridge and pasture, and showed me the fairy forts. One of the biggest was behind my cottage; he'd pointed out the shortest route. Was it worth seeing? It depended on what I was looking for, he'd said. A woman in sturdy shoes marched past my window with a basket of eggs.

When Padraic came at dark, his knock surprised me. I had heard no car. To avoid gossip, he'd parked down by the pub and walked. Sligo and Rosses Point were really one small town, he said. We shared a pot of good black Irish tea with cream, and Jameson's whiskey on the side.

The Third Policeman was lying on the bed. He put it carefully to one side and lay down. He seemed self-conscious as we got undressed. His skin was the palest white, almost blue and translucent, with a mass of freckles on his back and arms. He was thin with the musculature of a runner gone slack with lack of exercise. Hours we spent in the dark, he was a tender and considerate lover.

The full moon shone in the back window when he got up. He wanted to leave before the pubs let out and his car was recognized. The tide was up. The waves were crashing on the shore of Coney Island, across the bay. His shadow blended in with the hedges as he hurried down the road.

I climbed behind the cottage at noon, past the cemetery and across the peninsula between Sligo Bay and Drumcliffe Bay. I was trying to transfer the grocer's map onto the land before me. Historians said the ring forts, stone circles on the hilltops, were ancient earthworks of the lake people who had lived here five thousand years ago. The fairy forts remained as bits of wildness in the middle of pastures and planted fields. The farmers were reluctant to cut them down.

Rain clouds scudding overhead made the whole land mass seem like a ship heading out to sea. To the north crouched Ben Bulben, facing the waves; across the south was a sleeping woman stretched out in the Ox Bow mountains. Below were potato fields interspersed with neatly fenced pastures, each with its separate herd of cows. The only possible fairy fort would be the wild bushes on the hill across the way.

Climbing along the fence line, I reached a riotous heap of brambles. Blackberry canes, thorn bushes, and prickly shrubs were woven into an impenetrable green mass crowning the hill. Walking around it, I found an oval opening in the green wall with two flat white stones in front, like a doorstep and a sill. The entrance was framed by two small thorn trees with arching branches. At the doorstep a patch of wild columbines waved in the wind.

The hole was as high as a large dog. On my hands and knees, like the medieval drawing of the alchemist thrusting his body through the starry sky to the universe beyond, I poked my head in. A neat dark tunnel led under the brambles, too small for me to crawl through. Who had made the passageway, and who used it? Clearly it was in use. A runaway calf perhaps, or cattle squeezing in out of the rain, or wildlife seeking cover. Or maybe something else.

Down the far side of the hill was a small lake and what looked like a narrow stone path from the fairy fort to the edge of the water. I imagined a procession of little people in the moonlight. They danced and laughed as they made their way and chattered with those around them. Their faces glowed as they trooped down the road and disappeared into the water. I sat on the tiny step and smiled. In fact, I had seen nothing. But the road and the doorway indicated they had picked a perfect spot.

It started drizzling. I climbed beyond the lake toward Drumcliffe Bay to gain the highway and catch a ride, but there was no traffic. I walked an hour before the first car stopped; we reached Sligo by nightfall. Crossing the bridge, I ran into Padraic. The collar of his pea coat was turned up against the rain. Wisps of hair stood out beneath his cap.

"Why don't you go down to the pub?" he said. "I've some errands to do, but Kathleen's there. I think you'd like her."

"Did you tell her about the time we spent?"

"I didn't need to. She knew."

"Do you think she'll like *me*?"

"She's the one asked to invite you."

The bar was dimly lit. Four people were sitting where I had sat, at the end by the sink. Kathleen had her back to the door. When I sat at the opposite end, she turned around.

"Padraic says you're a writer."

I nodded.

"And what are you writing about?"

"I'm not. I'm walking around. I'll have a Smithwick's, please."

She poured a pint of the frothy ale and set it down.

"I've just come from the fairy fort above Rosses Point," I said. "I love the magic of the land here."

"And the people—you love them, too."

There was no getting around it.

"Absolutely. Are you angry?"

"Not at all. You made him happy. I don't."

Her face was framed by her lanky hair. Even disheveled she was amazingly beautiful—not regular features and a straight nose, but an intensity and slow-moving grace that informed her gestures.

"Maybe you're not happy yourself."

The four men at the end called for another round. She bantered with them as she poured their drinks. She appeared so vulnerable, but her jibes were pointed, deadly. She was like a baby in a bullet-proof vest.

"Catch." She sent the Guinness whizzing down the bar.

Center stage against the lot of them, she sent rapid-fire comments that had more than a touch of comic genius. Her tactic was to draw someone out, annihilate him with laughter at his own expense, appear to forget the whole game, then draw another out, and so on. When she looked my way, it was the glance of a confidante and sister, honest and alive. New customers came in and fueled the fire. It was as if I were watching two separate people performing brilliantly in one body.

When the pub emptied out at ten, she sat opposite me across the bar.

"When did you leave the stage?" I said.

"Years ago, when the kids came."

"Most people don't even know about the passion you have. They either haven't discovered it in themselves, or would be afraid to use it if they had."

She nodded.

"But if you don't get yourself back on a stage, you'll eat yourself alive. Family, friends, lovers, drink—that's enough for some people, but not you. I don't even know why I'm saying this."

"Because you recognize me," she tilted her head back and peered through the cigarette smoke, "and you're not afraid. Most women who come to this bar hate me. They hate how I can take their men, how I'm not afraid to."

"Hey look," I said, "it's not easy anywhere to stand up as a woman or an artist. You're holding something most people would pay money for, but it has its price. You've got to use it."

Padraic came in. He went around the bar and stood next to her. There were no customers left. The kids were sleeping at her mother's again. They invited me to stay the night. As we filed up the stairs he briefly caught her hand in his, and she pulled away.

Their apartment did not looked lived in; there were no homey touches, no things strewn about. In the living room were a couple of chairs, a couch, a green shaggy rug. Padraic put on a recording of Ornette Coleman in Stockholm.

Suddenly Kathleen jumped up. She changed the record to Django Reinhart, the great jazz guitarist in Paris in the 1940s. She grabbed a pillow from the couch; holding it to her stomach, she began to writhe. At first I thought she was miming the erotic moves of a burlesque dancer, but then I saw she was serious. She rolled onto the couch and then the floor. Her back snaked along the rug, the soles of her bare feet turned up into the air. She hugged the pillow in an isolated ecstasy that seemed to hover just at the edge of orgasm as we sat there. It was enthralling and exhausting to watch.

I took in the three of us—one performer and two witnesses. She needed an audience to stay at her pitch of frenzy, needed us to keep going, so I went to the bathroom. Returning, I saw Padraic had turned his chair away from her, but his face wore the saddest expression as he watched her writhing at his feet. She had pushed the pillow down, her eyes were closed, her lips smiling.

There was a childish ferocity in the dance. While she was at it, we couldn't carry on a conversation or pour a drink. We were locked in. Padraic knelt down to pick her up, but she pushed him away. She reminded me of a cartoon I had seen once of a tiny baby in a crib in the exposed cross-section of a house. The baby was in a bedroom, and the caption said: "The baby grew." In the next frame, the baby and the crib were as big as the bedroom: "And grew." In the last frame, the baby and crib had ballooned out, filling all the space from the basement to the rafters of the house: "And grew." The baby grew but did not grow up. There was no space left to breathe in the room where Kathleen danced. She had taken all the air out.

I decided to go to bed. I wasn't tired or even drunk. I just couldn't watch a second longer. Padraic showed me to his son's room. We held each other in the dark.

"Well, now you've seen her dance."

"Does she do it a lot?"

"Often enough."

"You're her lover and her friend, Padraic. From here it's the madhouse or the jail. She needs your presence to do that dance, it fuels her. Help her get back into the theater, or you'll be holding on to the threads of someone who just jumped off the edge."

I wrote in my journal: "Where are we different, Kathleen and I? In both of us there's a willfulness that would give it all up in a second for love, or work, or battle—something that can engage us fully. But warring with herself she has become a crippled Maeve. Where are we different? Mainly I have my writing, I have my work."

Traveling from Dublin to LeHavre, I sat in the deck chair and watched the constellations move up the eastern sky into the cloud cover. The pillow of light on the horizon was the moon, about to rise. I worked in the semi-darkness on the poems I'd written—songs of the Goddess in all the aspects I'd encountered. The raucous night I'd planned to have aboard ship I spent in solitude. It wasn't the Mother I was looking for, it was myself.

To come back to a city after fifteen years—where I had lived and worked, ferociously in love, published my first work, and given my first reading—and to find none of my landmarks was a shock. Vertically, Paris had grown; the skyscrapers obscured familiar neighborhoods. Rodin's statue of Balzac seemed to have moved from the place I remembered, near La Grande Chaumière. One little alley I'd lived in, by Boulevard St. Germain, had apparently disappeared.

In the Montparnasse Cemetery I looked for Apollinaire's grave, and found some stone booths with plastic flowers, and the headstone of Baudelaire. A passing couple told me Apollinaire was buried in Père Lachaise. I watched them walk away from me hand in hand; they seemed very much in love.

I sat at a table outside Le Dôme Café. A short fat man flashing a wad of franc notes propositioned me. Evidently he thought I was working. With his smiling teeth and the worried expression in his eyes, he looked like a chipmunk. It might have been funny, but in my heart I felt like an exile.

Walking back to my friend Sandor's place on the Right Bank where I was staying, I crossed the Seine under the wings of clouds lit up by sunset. I realized all the prayers I had prayed in that city—the fervent requests of a young girl for more understanding with her lover, more work, more money—had all been to a male deity. The father, the lover, Jehovah, or Jesus. Now all the signposts had been swept away. Those prayers no longer served.

Sandor, whom I'd known since my first time in Paris, was gay, as was his whole network of friends. In the sexiest of cities I was coming home every night alone. He advised me to cruise the streets, or sit down at a cafe and wait until someone I liked sat down to join me. I had a twilight encounter with a middle-aged Armenian rug merchant, who didn't know what to do or say. After a coffee we fled from each other in opposite directions down the street.

Sandor cooked us dinner one night in the miniscule kitchen of his postage-stamp duplex apartment. It was located, he liked to point out, behind the horse's hindquarters of the Sun King statue at Place de Victoire. Both floors were the size of a largish bathroom. The entire back wall on the top floor was covered with a gilded mirror that reflected him perfectly as he busied about the meal.

Sandor was tall, dark, strikingly handsome, with a wonderful grace to his carriage, and terrifically vain. It was hard not to know what you looked like at all times in his place. The love he had for himself had a nourishing all-forgiving quality, like the love of a father for his own child, and he moved with the languid air of an aristocrat, or a prodigal son. He was one of my closest friends.

"I can't believe," I said, "knowing half of Paris as you do, that after four days you don't have one straight friend to introduce me to."

His profile caught in the mirror behind him as he turned.

"None of *my* friends, dear, but you haven't met my cousin, Cal. A distant cousin, really, but that's reason enough for an introduction."

He ladled out vegetable soup at the table.

"We're so unlike each other, Caleb and I. He's family, and I love him of course, but I'm afraid he doesn't approve of my life style."

"Doesn't like being related to the Princess of Paris?"

"Oh, I'm sure he doesn't know. We don't talk about personal matters, and we don't meet often. But I think you might like each other. I'll call him up."

I took the early train from Paris leaving for Chartres and points west. Talking with the man next to me, I realized my French was coming back. I could leap beyond the commonplace to things I really wanted to say, albeit with enough grammatical errors to make him wince, but understand me, nonetheless. When I described my journey, he asked jocularly if I were *une païenne,* a word I had never known. A pagan. I gave him my imitation of a Gallic shrug.

The September countryside was golden brown and red at the edges. Coming in from the brilliant day to the relative gloom of Chartres Cathedral, I stepped onto a labyrinth about thirty-five feet across made of stone tiles. Much more complicated than the farmer's maze in the Glastonbury hayfield, the pathway made thirty-two turns around the circle before attaining the center, which was a six petal flower. Tracing my way in, I found the first quarter turn came nearest to the center before widening out to cover the entire surface. In completing the labyrinth, or threading the maze, perhaps one started out closest to what one desired before undertaking the arduous task of reaching it.

Chartres Cathedral was built in the 1100s over a site of Goddess worship already ancient when the Romans arrived. It was sacred ground, Caesar wrote, where people gathered once a year, and those with disputes accepted the decisions the Druids handed down. The Druidic sanctuary contained a spring the Romans then enclosed as a well. Nearby was a statue of the Mother Goddess in the act of giving birth.

When the early Christians found the Gallic people worshiping the statue, they declared her a prefiguration of the Virgin. They informed the Gauls that they were already Christians; without knowing it, they'd been worshiping Mary. One church succeeded another, and the statue remained in its original place, near the well. As the surrounding land rose with time, she became known as Nôtre Dame de Sous Terre, Our Lady Underground. In the anti-Church zeal of the French Revolution, the venerable statue was destroyed. Later, it was replaced by a more chaste version of the same mother seated, with her child already born.

A friend had told me if I stood in the Cathedral exactly where the nave and transept crossed, I would be standing directly above the underground intersection of two rivers. She said I could use myself as a divining rod, to find which direction the principal river flowed. I came to the spot before the altar, planted my feet, and closed my eyes. I found myself drifting right to left, north to south. Then I turned, facing the main entrance. My body moved left to right, again north to south. My friend had been right. The power of the current under the ground was alive in the air as well.

I made my way toward an alcove in the south transept which seemed to be the center of activity. A black Madonna dressed in gold brocade was holding her baby in her left arm. She was standing on a pillar surrounded by candles and flowers. A continuous line of people passed before her—nuns, old women, mothers with their daughters. One woman reached up and lovingly touched the hem of her gown. I thought of the Black Virgin of Copacabana in Bolivia, who was loved for her miracles of healing, and the Virgin of Poland; the black Goddess Kali, and the black-robed Isis. Black was so eminently suitable to the queen of the night.

I knelt in one of the pews and found myself unexpectedly crying into my hands with relief, with gratitude. It wasn't the statue, but something in the place itself. I felt comforted and renewed, as though my heart were healed. Alternately, I felt rather silly blubbering before a crowd of strangers, until I spotted several people doing the same thing. I rested in the calm and quiet until the next tour started for the crypt below.

In the dim light of the underground vault, our tour group visited the new statue of Our Lady Underground, a seated mother carved in wood, holding her baby in her lap. Our guide said she was placed directly beneath the Black Virgin in the alcove above. She said the ancient well was as deep beneath the earth as the spires were high above it.

I waited until the group passed on, and stopped for a moment. I put my hands on the sides of the well. Coolness came from deep below. The ancient mother had sat on her throne and had been worshiped by people who sang her name right where I stood. There were no bodies buried in the walls of Chartres. There were no monuments to war or to the slaying of dragons. The place had always been devoted to life, the mother of life under many names, including Mary.

I returned to the Virgin of the Pillar, and closed my eyes. When I opened them, a man was kneeling in the pew before me—a workman in rough clothes, weeping into his calloused hands.

The "family meeting" had been set for seven. When Caleb entered the mirrored room at Sandor's, he had to stoop down. Tall and gaunt with long thin hands, he looked like an El Greco ascetic. After very few minutes I recognized his black humor and the wolfish laughter behind his eyes. I liked him immediately.

During the drinks and small talk, I could feel Sandor monitoring our meeting. At exactly the proper moment, he got a call from someone, obviously a lover who'd just returned after a long absence. I loved the way Sandor had set it up. When he hung up, he apologized for not being able to join us, if we were going out. Caleb immediately invited me to dinner.

It was a rainy night. After dinner we went from café to café on the Left Bank. In The Old Navy on St. Germain we held hands, closing ranks against an obdurate drunk who kept demanding someone listen to him. Caleb suggested we go to his place. At his apartment he showed me photos of Sandor and him as children somewhere in the countryside of France. It wasn't the photos I was interested in; neither was he. He looked at me squarely and said we had three days to make love, and do whatever we wanted. Three days to do it all. Then he had to return to his life, his work, his child.

He was enormously tender and ferocious. Something about him reminded me of Fernando, of our making love in that city; all my vulnerability and trust, which that love had engendered, were touched anew. We went to sleep at eight in the morning and awoke at three in the afternoon.

Caleb was a Jew. In the driving rain over the Rue Mouffetard, he told me it was Rosh Hashanah. Coming back from the market with fresh fruit and vegetables for dinner, we saw a rainbow appear over his street. Seen against the gray bricks of his building, it seemed to land on his balcony. In the shelter of his apartment we consumed each other with glance, word, touch, all the senses eager and alive. Out in the Quarter, we were extraordinarily ordinary lovers. He held the back of my neck as we crossed the street.

All the places I had sought without success on first arriving we found together: the American Center, Balzac's statue, the Tour St. Jacques, the Musée Pompidou, and the Café de Lilas, where the absinthe-drinking poets had sat at the dark wooden tables, getting plastered. When I mentioned I'd looked for Apollinaire at Montparnasse and hadn't found him, Caleb laughed.

"The place was right, but the poet is another one. It's César Vallejo who is there. Let's visit him."

He led the way through the gates of the cemetery in the late afternoon. On the gray marble headstone of César Vallejo, there was one line engraved at the bottom:

"J'ai tant neigé pour que tu dormes."

We were sitting on opposite sides of the stone. He pointed to the inscription.

"It was written by his wife, Georgette, who is mad as a goat."

I read it as something like, "It is snowing in my heart because you are sleeping."

He chuckled. "No, it's not *because* you sleep, but *so that* you sleep. 'I have snowed so much so that you sleep. My hair has gotten white as snow so that you sleep in this bourgeois cemetery, where I have labored to find a place for you.'"

He waited for my reaction.

"But that's horrible!"

"Of course it is. The best poet of Peru, one of the best poets in the twentieth century, and no mention of it on his stone. No poem of his! Not even:

> I will die in Paris, on a rainy day,
> a day I already remember.

I will die in Paris—and I don't run from it—
perhaps a Thursday, like today, in autumn."

He tapped the stone. "You know, he actually lost consciousness on a Thursday, and died the next day. And it was raining, just as he said."

"Why do you want to keep it only in the present?" I said.

I caught his vulnerability and surprise.

"It's my way of holding it at a distance," he admitted. "At heart I'm a cold-hearted observer. What we're doing fits so easily it scares me. And it makes me want more. If it's in the present, I can have as much as I want."

"Okay, I agree we couldn't live this way. I mean no one could do it with this intensity, hour after hour..."

His mouth went up in a lopsided grin. "It would kill us." He looked around at the tombstones. "You know what I don't like about graveyards? The slabs are too small. How can a person my size make love on a tiny couch like that?"

We walked back to the car through the fallen leaves. He recited more of Vallejo, I recited Apollinaire. Crossing the Boulevard Montparnasse, he kissed my hand.

It's one thing to accept a time limit when you start; it's another when you're at the end. The following day Caleb would pick up his daughter, bring her to school, and go to work himself. Late that night, after we had made love and he was sleeping, I sat at the foot of the bed. I leaned over my knees in the lamplight and looked at the floor. In the cup of water at my feet I could see the reflection of the same solitary person who had walked in, walking away. It wasn't sad or happy; it was a fact.

Sandor was surprised to see me opening his door at the early hour of nine a.m.

"People from England have been trying to reach you. They want you to read somewhere in London this week."

I called and found it was a poetry festival. I'd been invited to read with a group of poets in Westminster Abbey. I immediately thought of calling Caleb and inviting him to come. In London I'd be at home with the language; I'd be able to show *him* around. We could have another day together, maybe two. I could even come back to Paris, maybe, and change my ticket home to a later date.

I looked at Sandor across the room. He had his reading glasses on, and was talleying expenses from his last job. Through all the years I'd known him, he'd always seemed to be a cross between a prince and a simple monk.

"Do you think, Sandor, afraid as I am to let something go, I could get the courage I needed if I asked?"

Looking over the top of his glasses was the monk.

"Courage is a solitary thing. All great decisions require it."

We sat in silence for a while.

"I hate to think of traveling alone just now."

He took off his glasses, laid them on the table, and regarded his reflection in the mirror.

"I haven't seen the Thames in more than a year. I could use a few days off. Will I do?"

I could have hugged him. "Of course, you're perfect."

The night was clear over London; a crescent moon was just visible over the traffic and bustling streets. Presenting myself at the Abbey, I was led through a labyrinth of rooms to the Chambers of the Dean, where the poets were gathered. Of the nine poets besides myself, I knew only Gregory Corso, whose work I loved. I respected the regard he had for his service to the muse as the serious and peculiar business of speaking for the truth.

The event was called Poetry Olympics. Writers from seven countries would read their work and the work of others among the tombs and plaques in the Poets' Corner to rekindle an interest in and love for the muse. The host was poet Michael Horovitz, a tall thin man with frenetic energy. He gave us each a copy of the program. Except for the three stars of the show—Corso from the

United States, Linton Kwesi Johnson from Jamaica, and British punk poet John Cooper Clarke, all of whom had large followings in London—we were to read for just five minutes apiece.

We went out into the glare of the spotlights and television cameras. About five hundred people packed the Poets' Corner. Looking over the crowd, I found Sandor leaning elegantly against a wall in his black Yves St. Laurent cape. He gave me a little wave with his fingers.

The poets before me went on longer than scheduled. When my turn came, Michael emphatically held up five fingers. I looked up at the arches sheltering all those celebrated dragon slayers. Of all the churches empty of a female presence, the protestant churches were the most bereft. The Dean of the Abbey, resplendent in his red robe, sat in the front row with his hands folded placidly in his lap. Corso sat on the other side, furiously smoking a cigarette. Here and there in the crowd were the green and purple hairdos of the punk fans, awaiting their poet.

I read my poems of the owl woman and the squatting mother, and gathered momentum. I looked at the people and sang to the dragon in her lair of stars, the Goddess as lover among the cafés, and Lilith the Queen. When I finished there was applause. I took my seat, and the camera zoomed in on Anne Stevenson, an English poet, who read about birds.

Nothing had changed. All the statues were still in place. The seismic shudder I had hoped would shake the stones and walled-up bodies of the enemy stronghold was imperceptible. The arches were magnificently unmoved. What I wanted wasn't destruction so much as transformation. I wanted the fire of the old faith rekindled from the inside out, starting with the heart, starting with my own.

I thought of Juan Ramón Jiménez's poem about the boat:

> I have a feeling that my boat
> has struck, down there in the depths,

against a great thing.
                                    And nothing
happens! Nothing. . . Silence. . . Waves. . .

Nothing happens? Or has everything happened,
and are we standing now calmly in the new way?

I would have loved to see everybody suddenly get up and dance around in a great circle with their eyes shining and their hearts full. But that didn't happen. Nothing did. Or had everything happened, as Jiménez said?

Atalaya

I've always been afraid of the jungle. The velocity of the life cycle frightens me: one could drown in that vortex. In the woods of the Northeast, where I live, it takes a week for an animal to disappear into the bellies of coy-dog, bobcat, fox, and crow. In the jungle it takes a day, and long lines of insects polish off what's left in minutes. My preference has always been mountains, where visible distance gives the space I need, both inside and outside.

One year, en route to hiking the Andes, I stayed on in Lima, Peru, long enough to gather information for a piece I was working on about the prisons there. I found access much easier than in the United States. Arriving with my passport at the prescribed hour for women visitors, no one even asked whom I wanted to visit.

The patio was crowded with hundreds of women, both visitors and inmates, under a cloudy sky and the watchful eyes of the guard on the roof with a machine gun. Someone found the women whose names I had; they were willing to tell me their stories, and were quick to point out that the garden in which we sat bore no resemblance to the *real* Chorillos prison, inside. We sat talking on a cement wall when a tall blond woman came out onto the patio and threaded her way through the sea of people.

I called out to her in English and she turned around. Despite the constraint in her face, she was beautiful. Her name was Lena and she was Canadian. As we walked back and forth across the patio, she told me she'd been arrested along with her boyfriend, Bert, for smuggling. She hadn't been involved herself, but her relationship with him made her guilty of complicity.

We talked until the guards on the rooftops started blowing their whistles. Visiting hours were over. I told her I was going to the mountains and asked if there was anything she wanted me to bring when I returned.

Lena shook her head. "Nothing, really. Until I go up before the judge, there's not much to do but wait."

"Come on, there's got to be something you'd like."

"Well, maybe a piece of fruit."

I returned a month later.

"That last time you were here," she said, "I talked for the first time in months. I felt alive and open. I felt human. But that's dangerous in here, where I could get killed over nothing. So I took great care to close myself up again. I didn't want to allow myself hope, not even for a pair of oranges."

Our friendship was cemented there. After I returned to North America, we kept up a correspondence. She was sentenced to seven years. When she received permission to marry her boyfriend, they were transferred together to Sepa, a penal colony in the Amazon jungle. After four years they were paroled from the colony, but were not permitted to leave the jungle province. With family help, they bought a piece of land down river from the prison, and planned to build a *fondo,* a working farm, on the Urubamba river.

Her letters were full of the animals and birds, and the astonishing vegetation. She described spending hours immersed in the chortling, humming, croaking, squealing, roaring, buzzing sounds around her. How she sat by the river alive in the moment, without a future or a past: a meditation she called "watching the river."

The name of the nearest town was Atalaya. I recalled the magazine I'd seen Jehovah's Witnesses give out at the subway stops in Spanish Harlem. Atalaya meant watchtower. She invited me to see her farm, and sent detailed directions. Since I had been twice to the Amazon, and had fled both times in fear of being sucked in and buried alive, I said I would try to come, but couldn't promise.

It was a gray day in the courtyard of Don Simeon's hotel. A little baby was being rocked in her hammock. The mother hen and her bevy of chicks left crosshatchings in the mud. A giant iron wheel leaned against the mango tree in the courtyard, open to the sky and the rain. Smoking a cigarette I did not want, I was trying to think.

Where had we gone the night before? The disco club could have been a soccer field, a wooden platform for a dance floor laid across the mud. Each straw-roofed cabana had held its own private party, illumined by greenish white fluorescent lights. The music was loud disco rock, and *chicha,* the pop music with a vaguely Latin beat. At eleven o'clock, the town generator stopped, and lights went off abruptly all over town. The starry sky had turned to lowering darkness. We'd had a lot to drink, and as we made our way down the hill, it started to rain.

Eduardo was so much smaller than I — diminutive almost — but I'd enjoyed his way of managing things, of directing his boat and business affairs, which I'd watched all day on the river. He grabbed my hand, and we laughed when the rain turned torrential. We had already gotten soaked coming down river in the storm the day before.

"Do I detect a pattern here?" I said. "You ought to change your name to Noah."

That was when we fell into the ditch. It must've been three feet deep. He fell on top of me and kissed me on the mouth. We struggled out of the hole in the downpour, slipping and sliding in the mud. Before us was a large ramshackle structure that looked like a barn or a warehouse. A small light was traveling through the cracks in the weathered wood. Someone was walking inside with a candle, probably going to bed.

"Let's wait here under the eaves," he said.

He pushed me against the barn, pulling at my clothes. The idea excited me — to make love in the mud, in the dark, with a man I'd been watching all day. My clothes were drenched. Moving together, our bodies made a slapping noise before they hit the wood. The rickety barn siding creaked; the person inside with the candle grumbled at the noise. We giggled, and the rain fell harder.

"You make too much noise," he said.

"It's not my fault if the walls are creaking. Why don't they build things more solidly here?"

We slipped and slid our way down the hill. Soaking wet, we reached his hotel. We made love in the pitch dark and broke his bed, but it wasn't as exciting as doing it in the mud. I took out my contact lenses and dropped them into the separate caps of two deodorant bottles in Eduardo's bathroom. Since there was no water coming from the tap, I filled the caps from the back of the toilet.

The next morning there was still no water. The rent I paid at Don Simeon's was cheaper because the one bathroom and shower were out on the patio and common to all. But they seemed to always have water. At Eduardo's hotel everyone's bathroom was private and evidently useless in dry season.

I surveyed the dreary mess of my clothes, and considered how I could cross the gossipy town square in broad daylight, covered in mud, without my glasses on to define the enemy. I washed my shoes in the toilet tank. Marching resolutely across the plaza, I held the deodorant caps before me like a tea tray.

I had come to Atalaya via Búfalo and boat. Búfalo was the Peruvian Air Force plane that serviced the jungle provinces, when weather permitted, bringing in passengers and supplies. The fare was cheap. The officer in charge reminded me, when I complained, that it was the people's plane: no frills, no padding, no seats, no pressure control. The wooden benches running down both sides of the bare hull were jammed with travelers.

It was like an Andean bus in the sky—with chickens, homemade packages sewn together, workmen with tools, women in colorful skirts, great sacks of produce, and a solidarity among the passengers born of shared hardship. At the highest altitude we were given a tube connected to an oxygen tank to breathe from and prevent *soroche,* altitude sickness. One woman was throwing up into a rag, which made all of us on that side of the plane queasy.

My fare was paid all the way to Atalaya, but the people aboard advised me to get off in Sepahua, which was just a short boat trip away from Lena's place. Landing, I stepped out with my pack into a hot humid blanket of air. Sepahua, I discovered, had an oil company and an army base. Neither had boats going down river that day. I resigned myself to a night in the airless closet that passed for a hotel room. One of the other lodgers, a beverage salesman, was bound for Atalaya in his boat the next day and offered me a ride.

By noon we'd arrived at Sepa, which was both penal colony and river control. Everyone passing the outpost was required to register in person. As we docked, the salesman remarked that Sepa had the latest weaponry and the fastest boats on the river. To his knowledge no prisoner had ever escaped. The officers were the ordinary bullies and petty tyrants one sees in outlying provinces— the sort who find entertainment in pulling copulating dogs apart, and laughing at them howl. They said Lena and Bert had left the area the week before, and had not returned.

Our next stop, a short way down the river, was a muddy embankment the salesman said was Lena and Bert's *fondo.* A caretaker came down and shouted that they weren't home. He waved down river to indicate where they'd gone. But down river was a big place; the entire Amazon basin lay that way.

Atalaya was situated on the lowest skirts of the eastern Andes, as the land dipped down to the Amazon rainforest. The slight elevation over the bottom land earned it the name "watchtower." The Urubamba and Tambo rivers joined at its northern end to form the river Ucayali, which flowed northward two hundred miles to Pucallpa. From there it ran to Iquitos, where it joined other rivers to become the Amazon.

I got a room at Don Simeon's hotel. Lena had written she always stayed there when she came to town. Everyone I asked of her whereabouts responded with the same vague gesture toward the river. Perhaps Pucallpa. Perhaps Iquitos.

I located Lena's godson, a boy of ten, who offered to show me around. I was in somewhat of a bind. Believing I'd be staying at Lena's, I'd left Lima with only a few traveler's checks. The two banks in town were on strike until further notice, so the boy brought me to a large hardware store on Ene Street that might be able to change them. All commerce stopped as I walked in. Both the customers and shop clerks listened to my request, and as if on cue, laughed uproariously. I hadn't realized I could be so funny.

The boy offered to walk me home. The heat in the dusty streets was overwhelming. Leaving me at Don Simeon's, he said someone was living there who knew me. I thought it rather unlikely that anyone I knew would voluntarily wind up in a place like Atalaya. We said goodbye.

Inside, at a long table under the roofed patio that faced the courtyard, a short dark man with intense eyes sat with a notebook opened before him. Don Simeon sat with him. I recounted my predicament. The short man, who introduced himself as David, said he might be able to help. After a pause, he said he had written to me once, inside a letter of Lena's. That meant he must've been in the penal colony with her and Bert, although I remembered nothing of what the letter had said.

My main occupation in the days that followed was inquiring after Lena in the Pucallpa hotels, and calling Lima for money. The telephone bounced a radio wave via satellite over the mountains, or broadcast over the river basin, but the line crackled and sputtered and often went dead. Meanwhile, David offered to show me the footpaths out of Atalaya. Since he was a *charapa,* jungle turtle, the name Peruvians used for those born in the jungle, he would be able to explain anything I wanted to know.

Walking to Yauyu, three kilometers away, David explained he had been the "cook" in a cocaine kitchen, and had gone to jail rather than give up the owner of the operation. But since his "graduation from the university," as he put it, he'd gotten into the lumber business, and worked his way up to foreman. Recently he'd gone out on his own with a six man crew, and specialized in mahogany. It was easier for a small operation to get up the narrower tributaries, and camp out in *selva dura,* deep jungle, until the rains came to float out the logs. Lena had told him I was a poet; he said he was a poet, too. There was an urgency about him I found unsettling.

When we returned to Don Simeon's, the newly hired boy said a blond woman with blue eyes had come to see me. She was staying in Don Juanito's, the other hotel. I grabbed the earrings I'd brought for Lena, and ran across the square.

I found Don Juanito in a chair by the window of his lobby. He was perhaps seventy-five years old and had, like everyone else I'd met in town, the habit of leaving his sentences half complete, and looking off at whatever happened to be passing—a chicken, a soldier, a leaf fluttering to the ground. I responded by leaning on things, and allowing for long pauses in the conversation, in the chance that something might still be said.

Don Juanito seemed to come swimming up from a great depth as he met my gaze. He said a gringa had just arrived that morning, and was staying at his hotel, but her name was Ingrid, and she'd gone—somewhere, lost to the present tense as he looked away.

Above us the tin roof held back the blast furnace and whiplashes of sun. David sat beside me, writing in a small notebook. The chickens were combing the yard again. Neither of us spoke. Perhaps in the jungle everything came down to a simple acceptance, or perhaps it was just I who accepted. Two people sat writing at the long table, and I was one of them. Tap tap tap. Simple declarative sentences. Everything was done in the open. You thought in the full light of day, surrounded by others.

Jungle life, I was learning, was composed of surfaces under and over and inside other surfaces. That morning, after an hour's sleep, I'd gone out to the bathroom on the patio. The usual army of flies had swarmed up in the small room—big black shiny flies that lived under the lip of the toilet bowl and flew down to the muck at the bottom. I tried to drown as many as I could with a pail of water. Then I straddled the bowl and squatted on the rim. Looking down, I was horrified to see three white maggots climbing up the slippery throat of the bowl. They were slowly advancing toward me. Surfaces inside surfaces. The advance guard of a transforming army in all the surfaces I could see.

The water had amoebas, but it felt good on my body in the slimy shower. With prayers against contamination, I brushed my teeth. Surfaces inside surfaces, and the constant slippery exchange of reality. I'd danced the night before with three or four men, but mostly with the young man I'd met in the telephone station. His name was Pancho, and I brought him back to my room after the dance was over. He looked like a lover I'd had in Paris, and though not as inventive, was adequate for someone so young. In any case, I was too drunk for it to matter much.

Around two or three, I went to the bathroom out on the patio. When I came back in, the candle was flickering on the table. I blew it out, and returned to the mattress we had placed on the floor. It was still dark. We continued making love. Pancho seemed much more daring and considerate and tender now.

Around dawn he said, "Do you know who you are with? I am David."

I opened my eyes, and looked at his face. It was David.

I couldn't believe it.

"How did this happen?"

"I came by before and your door was open, but you weren't here. So I took off my clothes and lay down. When you came back in, we made love."

"Are you kidding me?"

"Here I am."

"What happened to Pancho?"

"I never saw him."

It was David in bed with me, no question about that: David whom I'd avoided making love with because I felt he was too intense, too short, too needy and brooding.

I sat up in bed. "I'm completely confused. I need to be by myself for a while."

I made my way in the blistering heat at noon, to call Lima and Pucallpa again. It was so bright out I could hardly see. The telephone station was closed. A woman was standing in the middle of the road, back from the rank smell of the ditch in front of the station. She looked like she was waiting for someone. An American missionary, she was delighted to find I spoke English, and invited me back to her house for dinner.

She had a husband, three children, and two servants, all ardent Christians. Everyone sat together at the midday meal, and the talk turned to seeking the Lord within, of directing one's life toward spiritual growth. My confusion about David fell into the background as God hopped up on the table and strode purposefully over the cups and saucers. But my own acceptance of everything for what it was—surfaces inside surfaces—wasn't that growth? I promised to come back another day, and work with the children in their school at home.

Back on the patio at Don Simeon's, the chickens, rowdy from the heat, jumped up on the table. They pecked at my pockets. I bowed my head over the typewriter as the sun marched through the yard. I sat and rocked like the Jews, davening in the colors through the stained glass windows of Hadassah, outside Jerusalem.

Was my work a prayer, really? Was poetry a steadfast path of light? Or was it just the name for an excuse?

I was sitting in my new room, the best room in the hotel, right off the patio, the light streaming in from the yard, and a solid bed—a straw mattress on a wooden platform. A table, chair, and a couple of nails to hang clothes on completed the furnishings. David had traded it for my cavernous room down the hall, with its shipwrecked boat of a bed. He'd said what I really needed was a room I could feel at home in.

My ears were plugged against the music coming over the room partitions, three feet short of the hotel's tin roof. The one large room was like an army barracks divided into separate cubicles. The circulating air included sound. Intimate scenes were cloaked in radios, which was probably why so many played so loudly. No screams were allowed, no cries in the night. Because I'd ignored that rule the night of the dance, Don Simeon looked away whenever I caught his eye.

At six in the morning the radios began: *chicha* music, indecipherable news, lugubrious ballads, occasional salsa, pseudo-rock, and they lasted until late at night—a cacophony of radios worming their way through my earplugs. David and I were extremely careful. In our walks through town we maintained a strictly intellectual companionship. We avoided Calle Ene, the street of gossip, and walked the long way around the clumps of people with their talking hands and sidelong glances. The little restaurant down by the beach was the only place where no one cared who we were or what we did; we were welcome.

Once I'd settled into a room I enjoyed, I realized I wanted to share it. It was as simple as that. I invited David in to visit. We made love three times through torrential rains of a Sunday afternoon, when no walks were possible, no Sunday papers existed, and anyway it was the best thing to do.

I felt calm and quiet. I hadn't realized how much tension I'd been carrying. A wild energy had burst through me from my feet up. No amount of drinking could have kept it down. David was five inches shorter than me, and just as intense as I'd intuited. But the brooding quality I'd observed was a mask he wore to protect himself. He seemed an unusually open person with a healthy love of sex. There was a softness in his face as he lay on the bed behind me, reading. His hair was almost blue black in the stark light of the electric bulb.

The Urubamba and Tambo rivers, which joined at Atalaya to form the Ucayali, brought the constant commerce of small boat traffic. The beach was dotted with kiosks that catered to the boat trade: produce stands, bottle repositories, small cantinas, and restaurants. One of the thriving kiosks had a permanent wooden floor. Open to the air and the wind, Mélida's restaurant was a favorite with David and me.

Partitioned with sacks of beans and crates of beer, it had three wooden tables with benches for the customers, and a refrigerator that cooled beer and soda when the electricity worked. Behind the beer crates was the kitchen against the one standing wall, where three or four kerosene stoves were in constant service.

Mélida's world was hewn to fit the shape of her hands. Her husband, running about in his motorboat, returned with the produce, fish, and sometimes the mail. She wrung the necks of chickens and ducks, and cooked them with rice, beans, yucca, bananas, and occasionally greens. Her laugh was a rich throaty woman's laugh, set off by a gold tooth and dark amused eyes.

She surveyed her customers frankly, her hands on her hips. She was the local *huesero,* the bone doctor who set dislocated and broken bones, massaged injured backs, and wrapped ankles and knees. She could also tell fortunes by watching the configurations of burning paper and tobacco in two cigarettes she held and smoked together.

Her children ran around her, serving the beer and soda at meals, and setting the tables. They ran off to school in the morning with their book bags and did their homework in the evening on the wooden floor. Late at night, covered with a thin cotton blanket, they bedded down together across a few sacks on the floor while the adults talked.

One night, David and I went down to eat. Above the river were three planets—Mars, Saturn, and Jupiter—and a growing moon. Mélida came into the candlelight and sat next to her husband, joining us for a beer. My companions, all *charapas,* began talking of jungle spirits. Mélida said a baby's spirit would often stay inside the hammock where he had been rocked all day. If he were moved to another place, you had to take the hammock or his soul would not go with him, and the child would cry all night.

The *tunchi* in the jungle made a crying sound, but more like an animal's, so you'd be tempted to chase him, for the meat. That was him crying before it rained, because he didn't want to get his tail wet. He was large and, except for the tail, looked like a man. Once you got to where the sound was, it would have moved farther away. If the *tunchi* appeared as a bird and you shot him, you might see feathers falling, but when you got to the spot there would be nothing, the feathers would have disappeared. All this was to get you deeper and deeper into the jungle, where you would lose all sense of direction, and be lost forever.

The dolphin in the river was feared as well. When he came among people, he looked like a well dressed gringo with reddish hair. At weddings he often appeared as the bridegroom, and tried to carry the bride away. He would bring her to his underwater home. Sometimes she bore him a child that would grow up to serve him; sometimes she died, or he left her.

But he was a fabulous lover. Once with him the woman would refuse to leave the water, even if it meant that she would die. He frequently fell in love with women bathing alone in the river, and would do his utmost to entice them to swim away with him. Dolphins were called *bufeos,* and were famous for their love of play, but everyone respected them. No one ever killed the river dolphins.

We talked until late at night. No sounds came from the other ramshackle structures. The moon over Mélida's kiosk made a path that lit up the beach and cradled the eye on the water.

David had gone out to telephone places where we might find Lena. He reminded me of a friend I once saw glowing in the dark: he had the same sparks in the back of his eyes when he laughed. I imagined him sitting on the steps of the radio station. In the foul smelling air from the ditch he would be waiting for the door to open, or for his turn in line, or for the call to go through that never did. Not to Lima, nor the string of hotels in Pucallpa the radio operator had memorized. It amazed me that I might not see Lena after all.

Before I'd left Lima, I'd made arrangements to teach a writing class in Lurigancho, the men's prison outside Lima. I'd set the date for one month ahead. The prison was divided into separate buildings, and each building had its own libary — usually just a closet full of paperback books — and librarian. The librarians were the leaders in the literacy campaigns for prisoners. I was scheduled to teach at one of their monthly meetings, one week from today.

The disco music I hated was forcing its way through my earplugs. Buying fresh fruit in the market that morning, I'd heard a salsa tune. I suddenly longed to go back to Lima, to the world of the salsa dance floors and my lover in the band. The passion bottled up since I'd arrived in Peru was loose again — a large ambulatory animal that came and went, and carried away the places desire was answered.

I needed to own the part of myself that was forced to whisper while the radios blared. The passionate woman I was out in the open was snake-like here, electric, curving down the hallways in the dark. I was looking for something. Though I could not say what it was, the moment of giving it up in the act of love came closest.

Quena music came in from another radio down the hall — bamboo flutes from the Andes, a sad sweet innocent tune. I thought of the missionary kids I'd taught that morning. They had brought back my love for children, all children. What about one of my own? At forty-three, I was not going about it with any orderly plans, and the cigarette I lit reminded me I was certainly cutting my chances. But my tenderness that blossomed with David was directed at all small things — chickens, puppies, the zebu calf in the fields, babies rocking in their animistic hammocks, and tiny butterflies flitting in the muddy road. I wanted to care for them all.

David and I were walking the long way around Calle Ene when I asked him his full name. There was so much about him I did not know.

"David Pasos Recuay," he said. "My parents are gone, and my brothers have moved to the city. I come from nowhere, and in six months, who knows where I will be?" He chuckled, "Certainly where no letter will reach me."

He pulled some leaves from a bush in someone's yard, and handed them to me. They had a hairiness, like comfrey leaves.

"Soak them, then wash in the water," he said, "for smooth skin." He looked at me. "You already know the mountains, but the *selva* still has so much to tell you. If it's the Mother you are in love with, as you say, you need to know her face here as well."

It had become our ongoing conversation. For years I'd scorned the jungle as too enclosed, too hot, with too much vulture death velocity, but my horror and impatience had become delight. After the prison workshop I'd have one month before my return to America. As much as I yearned to walk the Andes, David was right. Lena's invitation notwithstanding, wasn't that really the reason I'd come— to dive into the pulsating energy of the jungle, and claim it as my own?

Mélida had read my future the night before. Her knowledge seemed to crackle up from the roots of herself; she reminded me of a tree walking. She had lit two cigarettes, and squinted. She'd said my journey would be long and slow. Since the Búfalo was booked solid, and the gasoline shortage meant no small planes were coming in or out of Atalaya, I would go by boat to Ocopa, by van to Satipo, then by bus over the mountains to Lima.

"If I got the first plane back from Lima, I bet I could be here in ten days."

David grinned. We passed a group of people on the corner, and one man grabbed his arm. It was a friend. He'd just seen Lena in Pucallpa. She'd heard I was here, but had no money to travel, which was what David had said all along. So perhaps I might see her when I returned.

We reached Don Simeon's just as the lights came on. Out in the yard the little girls were taking showers under the hose. Someone wearing only a towel passed in the shadow of the mango tree. It was very much like Hawaii. Fires were lit for separate dinners all around the yard, and the grandmother was singing a lullaby to the baby laying on the table. The baby turned and looked at me sweetly. It would be so easy to stay right here and allow the jungle to show me what I wanted to know.

I thought of a friend living in Iquitos who was planning to build her own place in the forest. When she'd first come to Lima from America, she'd gone to the jungle and fallen in love with her tour guide. She got divorced, cashed in all her assets, sold her house, quit her job, and returned to the Amazon. At the time I couldn't believe it. A tour guide? But the truth was she'd fallen in love with a fecund quality in herself, and it changed her life. Where did love come from? Up from the earth. That was the lesson. Which didn't exactly eliminate my fear that perhaps next time it would not be so easy to extricate myself from the tender impenetrable web *la madre selva* wove in her own sweet time.

Eleven days later I returned. I'd had to wait out one day in Pucallpa, because of the rain. Don Simeon said David had waited ten days. When I had not arrived the day before, he'd gone up river with Lena and Bert, who had stopped in on their way home. There was no word on when they would return. I dropped my things in the room we had shared and walked down to the corner restaurant overlooking the river. A few dozen buzzards brooded over their cache of garbage on the river bank below.

I asked for the special of the day, and one of the women said it was fish. I nodded assent, and took my Coca Cola to the window seat. After an hour, I inquired about my order. The woman, surprised, said she'd thought I'd asked out of curiosity. My city pace came to a screeching halt. I was back in jungle time.

Walking around the town, I passed a plastic lawn chair facing an ancient vanity table at the entrance to someone's house. A pair of scissors was reflected in the mirror; there were piles of hair on the floor. I took the evidence of earlier customers as an indication of the hairdresser's skill and asked her for a haircut. She looked at my lengthening raggedy crewcut and asked what exactly I wanted; my hair seemed short enough to her. I told her to follow the existing line, and give me a trim. She went to work. Fifteen minutes later, I had a boot camp haircut. A forty-three year old woman got up with a twenty year old soldier's head.

I was sitting at the table in the courtyard, reduced to the simple equation: sex or no sex. My lover had left town. My bad humor surfaced in an angry gesture at the sleeping dogs. At the hairdresser I'd noticed how old I looked, and it all came down to the question: sex or not. Having it or not. Being radiantly alive or not.

I could take a three hour siesta, or go to a fiesta and dance my heart out; but my body was breaking down. The book I'd brought with me by José María Arguedas was *Todas Las Sangres, All the Bloods,* and that said it nicely. Sanitary napkins were thrown to the buzzards. All the bloods accumulated in one vessel were deliriously running out.

I didn't need to be shorter or younger or less experienced than the man I picked, but I did need to need him. I needed to own up to my own need squarely, face to face. I needed to enjoy myself at play. I was not David's woman, or anyone else's—not even my own. My passion exceeded ownership. The play was in how it pertained to no one in particular, but where I felt a response, a stirring. To what my eyes, lips, breasts, and vagina wanted. The play belonged in the present, with no past history of promises, vows, judgments or recriminations. Allowing myself to play was the hurdle, and the key to my own enjoyment.

But here I was, alone. The typewriter I loved so well was breaking down, the space bar stuck. The smoke from my cigarette was killing me. My haircut looked disastrous, and the lover I'd come to see was not in town. The chickens combed the yard—the little ones peeping and peeping—as the sun went down yellow green, and I was dying. Bleeding and dying.

Back in Atalaya I was ready to penetrate *selva dura,* hard jungle—the untouched deep recesses of the rainforest—accessible only by poling up the feeder streams in a small boat. But I discovered it wasn't possible to navigate those tributaries in dry season; there wasn't enough water. Bushwhacking up the ravines was not advisable either, without machete and rifle. The jaguars and ocelots were more than happy to welcome any interloper on their terrain. They saw it as lunch.

At twilight I walked down to the river. The luminous blue green light reminded me of the sky in one of Munch's paintings. In it a woman stood by a forest with her hands clasped behind her, watching the sunset through the trees. I caught sight of my friend Eduardo the boatman, eating with two friends in Mélida's kiosk. They introduced themselves, Cristóbal and Miguel, and invited me to listen to records.

People in the jungle speak of building with *materia noble,* a substance that will not break down or rot in the jungle rain. That noble material is usually cement. Cristóbal's home was a concrete bunker furnished with a wonderfully eclectic library and a warehouse of canned goods. I deduced from his books that Cristóbal was a student of esoteric wisdom.

The music was jazz. Miguel, the second friend, made frequent trips to the United States and had an extensive collection of American jazz. I'd learned my first week in Atalaya that almost everyone of substance in town was connected in some way to the cocaine business, and wanted somewhere by the law. Miguel's trips to Miami were probably more complicated than visiting Disney World and shopping for records.

As if on cue, Eduardo and Cristóbal left the room at the same time, and Miguel offered me some cocaine. I declined. He said he had genuine Irish whiskey at his house, which we could share if I went home with him. I said nothing. The other two came in. I went outside to take a pee, and Eduardo followed. While I hunkered down and looked at the stars, he offered to take me all the way up river to Lena's *fondo* the next morning, if I would return with him to his room. I said I didn't think so.

Back in the bunker, I was standing by the book shelves reading the titles, when Cristóbal came over and stood beside me. Under the cover of Stan Kenton's band, he said he could see I was unusually intelligent, and invited me to stay and talk after the others had gone. I shook my head.

Drinking liquor with the three of them, I reflected on their relative power and prosperity, and how it was no prevention or cure for their aloneness. They were kingpins in a macho society. Had any of them been feminists, there might have been women with them engaged in talk and laughter. If women had been allowed beyond the confines of their kitchens and homes, there would have been other women besides myself, and these men not so desperately alone. There was a certain ironic justice to it, which didn't fill my own need either for the company of women.

I went down to look at the river. There were no boats coming in. Venus was conjunct with the moon in Scorpio, and he wasn't coming. He'd gone up river with that notorious egocentric, Bert, who might keep him there for weeks.

Back in the courtyard the happy puppy scampered around my feet, and I burst into tears. In my room I tried to figure out why. It was the whole rotten scenario I was creating for myself. I had a caring attentive lover and I was trying to fit us into a time frame. I was not taking it one day at a time, like a journey into the unknown dark—the *selva dura* alive with possibilities. I was holding onto a circumstance, and simultaneously closing it down. To ward off possible loss, I was creating it. I was the mother who could not watch life frolic around her feet without the sense of terrible loss to come. Before saying hello I was crying at the good-bye up ahead. No wonder I kept smoking, creating a smoke screen over the vista I could not believe in.

The fluorescent lights were blinking on. Electricity surged to all the outlets, and the radio wars began right on schedule. The kids were starting a new game in the courtyard. And if David came back that moment and walked in the door? That was just the point. It would still be sad.

We would walk through a play already mapped out with stage directions, and grind on to the end. No matter where we went or what we did, good-bye would go with us like a third person; he'd divide himself in half at the end, and each of us would carry him back to our separate worlds. Good-bye was the trickster with all the faces, the last sad commerce between radiant hearts.

Going up river, the sky seemed higher and wider than any space available from shore. David, Bert, and I were heading south to Lena and Bert's *fondo*. Flocks of colored birds wheeled overhead. The clearcut areas along the shore had a desert aspect: stark ground cover over dusty earth. Hot weather trees. Just up from the river were occasional round wooden huts, built by tribesmen away from home fishing the river. Long thin boats traveled between Atalaya and Sepahua loaded down with drums of oil for sale.

In the Amazon basin planes crashed and roads were gobbled up by the jungle. Only the rivers were reliable highways. The Urubamba was wide enough for several lanes of traffic at once. A steady wind kept the insects at bay, and the pattern of high clouds mirrored the freedom I felt to be moving after days of inaction. David and I sat in the middle seat, next to the mound of supplies.

Bert, looking ahead for changing currents and trouble spots, sat in the prow. His boatman, a teenager from a nearby tribe, worked the tiller. Bert was an herbalist and naturalist who'd spent the better part of twenty years in South America traveling, observing, and living with the native people. He had the self-absorbed quality of someone distant from his own roots, who was still not part of the cultures he observed. Like most Americans he spoke Spanish poorly.

We arrived in late afternoon. A horde of tiny bugs attacked as soon as we reached shore. Called *la manta blanca,* the white blanket, they materialized out of nowhere when the wind died, and attacked all exposed body parts. I was told people swabbed themselves with kerosene to keep them off.

Lena came running down the path. I hadn't seen her in five years. Tall, blond hair, the same calm blue eyes. The angular tension I'd met in prison had not exactly disappeared, but softened. We embraced and looked at each other. We were the same height. She was younger than I by about six years. We could have been sisters.

Their *fondo* was an old Shell Oil camp, built to house and feed the drilling crews. The long building that had once been the barracks was divided into six smallish rooms in the front, and one enormous room in back. Two full-sized *guacamayos,* Lena's colorful parrots, had a little swing up near the rafters of the back room, where they slept at night.

All the other rooms were empty, except for the one they offered us, which had a bed. Their own bedroom, decorated with jungle weavings and mosquito netting, opened onto a smaller room Bert used for his medical supplies. David set to work at once, making the mosquito net we would need come nightfall.

Shaded by a high tin roof extending thirty feet out in front of the building, the "living area" would have made a good stage set. A large window had been cut into the wall, and was the counter for Bert's store. When the store was open, a hinged shutter swung up from the house and was propped up on two sticks, like an awning. Stocked with liquor, beer, cigarettes, sweets, canned fruits, and some local produce, the store catered to the guards at Sepa Penal Colony, and some intermittent river trade. In the screened window hung a scale, and a sign: CASH ONLY.

In front of the store was eight feet of wooden flooring and two low-slung canvas chairs. To the right was the wall to the generator shed, a long table and two benches. Stage left was a barrel of river water smelling a bit rank, and two wooden tables. The first held the basins for washing up after meals; the second, foodstuffs and condiments in jars and tins, and the tableware. The cement fire pit on the stamped earth was center stage. It held an iron grill and several pots; they sent waves of heat up to us as we walked past.

Outside the protection of the tin roof was the baked earth, a grove of yucca bushes, and two wash lines in the roaring sun. Beyond that was *el monte,* the bush. Not a hint of a breeze. The patio, even shaded, shimmered in the heat.

Out on the patio, night had fallen. The generator behind my shoulder roared like a locomotive going full tilt up a grade. The electricity it gave to run the three light bulbs seemed hardly worth it. The space bar on my typewriter only went to the middle of each line. My three companions were dancing on the wooden floor, each plugged into a separate Walkman, each dancing alone. It could have been a locked ward in any corner of the so-called civilized world.

I had walked that morning with David into the jungle. In the early light filtering through the canopy, a band of monkeys had screeched from one of the trees. Midway to the river behind the camp, I'd found a white and pink flower, and showed it to him. I'd said it was everything I was not — honest, open, and free to be itself, regardless of the consequences. He looked at me quizzically. Maybe I was exaggerating, but it seemed the closer we got to each other and the more I needed him, the less disinterest I could pretend. I wanted something from him. That was business. I didn't want to marry him. We would probably be horribly suited for each other. I wanted the sex, and the tenderness, and myself opened like a flower.

He stared at me, and shook his head, and said nothing.

Later that afternoon I had gone to the river again with Lena. I'd gotten bitten so many times the night before — my legs, arms, shoulders, neck — I was one itching envelope of flesh. The water was a cool relief. We swam in a deep pool under fist sized holes chiseled in the rock wall above us.

She said the river ran four feet higher in rainy season, and the cliff face was usually covered with water. A certain fish made the holes to lay their eggs. The oval slits looked like giant stone vaginas. The likeness was wonderful. Paddling in the water, we took turns reaching in with our hands.

"So when I picked that flower," I said, "I started to cry. I don't want to misrepresent myself. I love the attention, I love what I'm learning, but I don't want to hurt him. I don't want to get married."

Lena hooted, and slapped the water.

"Who's asking you to get married? The bugs have gotten to you, girl. Enjoy yourself. He is. David is a dreamer. Sometimes the things he thinks about himself are true, and sometimes they're just a dream. But so what? Do you feel guilty for having so much fun?"

"Does it show?"

"Did you think I thought you were studying Quechua?"

"He's amazing. He can make love five or six times a day."

"Mmmm, I wish I had that problem."

"What's with Bert?"

"We couldn't make love in jail because there was no privacy. Now he's out of practice."

"God, how do you manage in this heat?"

"Without going crazy? I keep myself busy."

"More power to you. I couldn't do it. It's so orgiastic — even the bugs — the only busy I'd keep is jumping on my hand." Our laughter had bounced off the rock wall, and echoed up the ravine.

Now, the generator was blaring behind me as my three companions danced in separate circles across the floor. The smell of rotten water wafted over the patio from the ditch in the yard. I swabbed calamine lotion on my skin in ever widening circles, then dabbed insect repellent on top. Neither one worked. My skin was too feverish to calm, and these bugs could eat through the Grand Coulee Dam.

We couldn't go out. Lena had lent me a pair of rubber thongs, but Bert told me I ought not walk off into the grass because of poisonous snakes. Everyone was walled off inside themselves. The mosquito net David made for our bed cut off all the air. There was nowhere to go.

Of the two rivers—the wide, fast-moving Urubamba in front of the *fondo,* or the little river behind—I preferred the latter. It was absolutely private, and since I was not much of a swimmer, it was more my size. I could leave all my clothes on the bank in the order I'd need, to dress again quickly once out in the air. As soon as I was in the water, the tiny swarming insects of *manta blanca* that burrowed under the skin and left huge itchy welts disappeared. Curiously, they didn't bother the face or scalp.

Up river from the pool by the rock wall was shallow water, barely enough to cover my body. I pulled myself along on my elbows like a crocodile, my eyes just above the water line. The *quebrada* narrowed above me. Fabulous birds flitted back and forth across the river. Gusts of wind shook the trees and sent down showers of dead leaves, blossoms, white tufts, seeds, and feathers. They floated toward me on the surface of the water in a stately and sweet procession. When the water became too shallow for cover, I turned around.

Coming back on the path through hallways of green light, I looked sharp and carried a machete. For all the talk of snakes, I never saw one. Monkeys screeched high overhead. The jungle floor was thick with leaf layers crunching underfoot. Some trees had put down three or four trunks to support their mass in the shallow soil.

Unlike the woods of North America, where only four or five trees predominate in an area, there were dozens of different species, impossible to differentiate and memorize. Some were blooming, some shedding their leaves. Lines of ants marched across the trail. In the proliferation of leaves, vines, ferns, fronds, bushes, webs, bugs and flowers, vision was confined to the near at hand. There were no distant views.

My days outside the water consisted in measuring the variations of heat in every environment, and seeking out the coolest spot. The yard was too hot to stand in for more time than it took to hang the wash. The patio baked under the tin roof; short gusts of wind were counterbalanced by the hot coals from the fire pit. Wasps swarmed out of their hiding place and frequently attacked.

With doors closed to the heat all day, the barracks built up a small storehouse of freshness. A quiet breeze sometimes crept through the opening under the roof. I often sat in the coolish dark until it was time for the river.

Lena said she had a dolphin in the Urubamba, who visited whenever she went swimming. I went down with her to the river. Planting my feet in the muddy bottom against the fast moving current, I washed my laundry while she swam. After fifteen minutes a dolphin appeared. He wasn't white or red as the story described. He was gray and appeared to be smiling.

He stayed about twenty yards from her, sporting and playing in the river. He leaped up and dived down again into the water. Perhaps he *was* in love with her, as the local lore would have it, and did want to carry her away. Perhaps he just considered her his friend. Either way, it was amazing to see him.

Heading back to the house, we detoured down to a banana patch carved out of the jungle, about a quarter mile from the river. Five minutes out of the water we were sweating again.

"You always refer to the dolphin as he," I said. "Maybe it's a she. Wouldn't that be just as good?"

Lena shook her head.

"It's this feeling I have, since the first time he came. With boats always passing, people always staring at *la gringa,* I have no privacy. The first time I dared to take all my clothes off and stay under the water, there he was— about thirty yards away. Now, almost every time I go to the river, he comes to see me. At first I was afraid. I mean, you know the stories. Dolphins are pretty big, and water is their world, but he never comes any closer. I feel sort of protected by his presence."

"You know what I feel?" I said. "You're lonely. There's some part of you that's not getting nourished. All that gentleness you couldn't show in prison needs a place to grow. What's with Bert? What *does* he do for you?"

We had stopped to look at a pair of butterflies with black and white 69s inside the fabulously red borders on their wings. They were flapping languidly on a rotten stump.

"We're not allowed to leave the jungle. Even in our own place we're not exactly free. He's having a hard time with the confinement. When he drinks too much it sets him back, but I know he's trying."

We'd arrived at the banana trees, but the bunches were too high for us to get, and neither of us had brought a machete. A band of monkeys set to screeching and hooting from a nearby tree. Lena called to them, and many chittered in response. She kept it up with them, call and answer, until they drifted away. I liked her proprietary air, pointing out the papaya trees, and telling me her plans for the land as we walked back to the house. We made our own choices. Who was I to judge?

Imprisonment in my envelope of flesh made normal sensuousness impossible. I carried a bottle of rubbing alcohol and cotton swabs Bert gave me wherever I went. At night I lay back waiting for the itching to begin. If David touched me, I pulled away. If he snuggled up to me in sleep, I rolled over. My ecstasy of scratching had turned the bites into festering sores. The least new lesion raised the hair on the back of my neck. I became obsessed with my skin.

One night I dreamt of my mother. She was surrounded by bottles of medicine against all diseases—medicines she would never have taken in real life. I dreamed she was imprisoned in a house of flies and filthy rags. To counteract a present given to me by my father, she handed me a gift. It was a tiny package of M&Ms, with which she hoped to recapture my love. Waking up, I saw the prison of rags was the place I was in, and I was my mother. It made me sad.

The open space between the wall partitions and the tin roof made every conversation audible to all. David had so little English he could turn it off, but I became an unwilling participant in the intimate scenes between Bert and Lena. I insisted our own love-making, mine and David's, be carried on in whispers. No rocking beds, no shouts or screams.

Lena's opinion that not all of David's dreams were true made me look coolly at his stories, and question their veracity. Did he really have a mahogany business and employ six men? He became less of a mythical figure. I was less willing to be swallowed whole. Our lovemaking was hot, but the thrill—aided by my own desire to lose myself in his eyes—had become more a conscious act.

Lena and Bert were travelers like me. I identified with them. But the openness of jungle life, brought to an apex in the shared barracks, made me seek out solitude. I didn't like the way Bert treated her. No matter how much he claimed to respect her, and love her good nature, he still ordered her around. I didn't like the old macho business-as-usual. On our second day at camp Bert had offered his opinion that men needed sex more than women.

"I can't believe we're the same age," I snapped, " and you still believe in that crap. Men need sex more than women? What a crock of shit! Sensuality is our province. Ask any woman. Or wouldn't we qualify with you as valid sources of knowledge?"

By the look on his face, I'd taken him by surprise. I respected Bert and I couldn't just dismiss him because I didn't like his style, but I couldn't keep quiet, either.

The fourth night, I broke down. I confessed to Bert that I hadn't taken a shit since my arrival. It was impossible for me to relax in the outhouse or anywhere else, day or night. I'd become too paranoid about bugs attacking me to let go. Bert looked up. His slender face, with the long graying hair pulled back in a ponytail, came alive in a mischievous grin.

"Why don't you spray your ass with Off? Spray your whole body from the waist down, if you want. Believe me, it works. Here, take my flashlight. Just relax and enjoy it."

I followed his advice, and it worked. Afterward, out of curiosity, I peered down the hole with the flashlight to the pool below. A giant green frog looked back at me from the edge of the muck. A hefty diet of buzzing flies agreed with him; he looked fat and cheerful. I dubbed him the patron saint of release.

Bert's rubbing alcohol was working also. My skin was becoming less feverish; I was beginning to relax. Lovemaking with David was on the rise. Down by the river in the morning, we swam together in the rock pool.

"You see," he said, "as a lover, I am very tender. I don't make demands. You might take that for a passive nature, but it's not. I like to know you're satisfied. It's just the way I am."

That night for the first time since our arrival, Lena and Bert made love. Every sigh was audible. David and I became co-conspirators, elbowing each other and rooting for orgasms. At last. Lying in the dark, I was glad for Lena, but I wouldn't have traded places for the world.

The heat, flies, and liquor at the camp brought an aimlessness and lassitude, augmented by the visits from the local guards of Sepa Penal Colony. Swaggerers and bullies, they came to buy beer, and exchange local gossip. Atalaya began to look more attractive every day. David and I were discussing hitching a ride down river, when someone docked below.

The man looked to be from a local tribe. Unlike everyone I'd observed coming up the path, he was neither drunk nor looking for liquor. The other striking thing about him was his eyes: they were open, clear, and they laughed. Without taking anything too seriously, he seemed to carry a center of gravity that was not easily moved. I liked him instantly.

Bert introduced us. Don Mateo was a *curandero* on the river who had prepared ayahuasca many times for Bert and his friends. Bert looked expectant; I understood he was asking if I wanted to try it. I trusted Don Mateo, and nodded assent. It was arranged for the following evening. Don Mateo instructed us to eat nothing after breakfast, and to come to his house at sundown with an empty stomach.

The following evening, Bert took David and me down the river to the *curandero's* house. Our arrangement had been so spur of the moment, I was surprised to find other boats docking. Since telephones were nonexistent, I wondered how so many people had gotten wind of the ceremony on such short notice.

Ayahuasca was used to cure physical diseases, or any problem one might have — mental, emotional, or spiritual. It was best taken in the dark of night, with little or no moon. Our moon was bright and growing, but Don Mateo said it was better than daylight, when the brightness could be overpowering, and the teachings lost.

Under the tin roof of the patio, Don Mateo spread a ground cloth over the dusty earth with great care. I had the feeling he was creating a space where he could hold and protect his charges through the night. Two apprentices brought in bunches of sweet basil and other herbs, and a block of wild jungle tobacco called *mapacho*. The *mapacho* was shredded and rolled into cigarettes. Everything was done with serious attention to details.

Don Mateo's daughter would take the drug with us. She had something wrong with one leg: perhaps polio, or severe arthritis; she seemed to be in pain. She wore all white. The rest of Don Mateo's family retired behind the walls of their house. Night fell.

We were twelve: David and I; the two apprentices, who were there to serve and to learn; Don Mateo's daughter; a young couple who were having trouble conceiving; an older woman and three men, who sat together; and lastly, a boy of perhaps ten who served in Don Mateo's household, and came from a nearby warrior tribe.

Flanked by his apprentices, Don Mateo sat with his back against the outside wall of his house. In front of him was a small table, on which was the ayahuasca he had just brewed, plus an assortment of bottles and flasks, various rattles and gourds, the herb bundles, and rolled cigarettes.

To his left sat the little boy, and next to him, with her back to the south, was Don Mateo's daughter, dressed as if for a wedding. David and I faced the *curandero* across the patio; our backs were to the river west of us, down the steep embankment. Next to us was the couple, who shared a blanket and presented themselves as a unit; then the older woman, and the men, with their backs to the north.

Ayahuasca, called *yage* in Colombia, meant death vine in Quechua. The hallucinogenic drink was made from the jungle vine, ayahuasca, *Banisteriopsis caapi,* which Don Mateo said grew far away from the sight of man; and the leaves of a forest shrub, chacruna, *Psychotria viridis,* which he called *la jocosa,* the comical lady. It was she who gave the journey its laughter. He said we could recognize her, if she appeared, as a very short, good-natured woman.

He gave each of us a glass of the brew to drink. The taste was a dark vegetable green, vaguely woody and bitter, but not unbearable. When he handed the glass to the boy, the boy shook his head.

"Why are you here in the circle?" asked Don Mateo.

"To watch."

"There are no watchers here, only participants."

The boy shrugged, and held out his hand for the glass.

Feeling nothing, after a time I asked for more of the potion. Don Mateo gave me another glassful. A bird began to sing in the dark. Don Mateo said her name was María. Her song sounded like *cocodrilo, cocodrilo.* He said she always came to the spirit of ayahuasca. There was an animal feeling in all of us huddled expectantly on the patio, like sheep grouping up at the barn door.

My own journey began. I was in a green cathedral, composed

of arches and muted colors lit from within. My emotions seesawed between reverence and merriment. All problems seemed nonexistent, almost laughable; all the states of being I might hold to, evanescent. A female presence was everywhere—in the leaves, the trunks of trees, the drops of water—fecund, pulsing, green and dark. The bird María came and went.

I flew out to the reaches of created worlds, worlds within worlds, where everything was round and returned along curves coming back to the body, again and again. The vast jungle, the vaster earth, star systems and galaxies were one round order that took form when it curved back to itself, as it always did. All expansion was followed by contraction.

Don Mateo entered into my journey. While I was traveling, he suddenly stood before me, like he had stepped into my dream. He appeared several times like that, as though he were inside my head. I couldn't tell if he could see what I saw or not. Part of me was aware of him doing the same with others. He was a maternal presence that did not close its eyes or waver in its attention to his charges. The flying lasted all night.

He came to each of us physically as well. He sang to *La Señora,* the mother of everything, over our heads. He rattled and waved sweet basil and wafted smoke our way with a woven rug. His moves were purposeful and calm. He sang the longest over his daughter's leg. So beautiful, she was the princess of the night.

The path of the waxing moon through the vegetation wove a net of cellular intricacy, like a three dimensional spider's web. Walking through it to go to the bathroom, I saw the truth of cellular integrity: how the life principle gathered blocks of matter around itself, and the light that ensouled it was the glue. Walking back through the shadows, I saw how all matter integrated with other matter, disintegrated, lost its individuality, then separated out into itself again. When anyone moved, they trailed a path of light behind them, like a comet.

Long after the moon set, Don Mateo lit a cigarette made from *mapacho* and gave it to each of us to smoke. From the free flight out in the air we were suddenly contracted down to our individual selves seated on the patio, stapled to the earth, seeing in the dark. There was an awareness among us, like a herd of cattle have resting in a field at night.

The *mapacho* cut into the journey. I was aware of my fingers, my shoulders, my lungs, myself pulsating in the dark. Don Mateo asked each of us separately if we were back. Another cigarette went around the circle. Harsh strong smoke. Everyone had landed.

People prepared to sleep in place for the few hours that remained of the night. The little boy very deliberately thrust his legs out in front of him and covered himself with a blanket. Visible in the outline of his body were his arms crossed resolutely over his chest. It was the stance of a warrior.

Before dawn people started leaving in twos and threes. The little boy disappeared. Don Mateo's daughter picked up her blanket and walked away. The light came blue gray through the green canopy. Only David and I were left. The *curandero* instructed us to take only water and eat nothing all day. He pointed to the stream behind his house and said we should wash our bodies and drink the water and take nothing else.

"The ayahuasca will keep teaching all day," he said. "It is important that you keep listening."

Behind his house was a herd of zebu cows making their way toward the fields. The little warrior was leading them. I noticed he had a goiter on his neck. His eyes sparkled and laughed. David and I went to a basin hollowed out in the stream. The water was a living presence, flowing over and over the skin of my body. One body on another body. Above was a *guayaba* tree with ripe yellow glowing fruit. We gathered a couple of dozen and carried them back to the house.

Don Mateo nodded at the fruit and said that night we could break our fast. His boat was ready to take us back. One of his apprentices sat at the tiller. The little warrior sat at the prow. His eyes were so sharp, he pointed out some turtle eggs on the shore, fifty yards away.

Once we were underway, the boy admitted that a great snake had come to him in the dark. The snake had been as large as the river. He had been very frightened but he hadn't screamed. He said this with a touch of pride. I thought ahead to my bags at the camp. I wanted to give him something for sharing his journey, something red.

Back at the *fondo* I handed him a red beaded bracelet woven in the snake design by a local tribe of Chapibos. When he put it on his wrist, he laughed delightedly. The bracelet seemed to be glowing, as was his arm. He and the apprentice waved goodbye. Trailing light behind them, they walked down to the dock.

David and I made our way to the little river through vegetation soaked with light. Something had opened. It was time to go, to set our sights on the Urubamba, and send out our intention to reach Atalaya. Intention was the telephone I had been looking for in the jungle. It was the arrow under the canopy roof that sought its mark, and more often than not found it.

We came back and packed in twenty minutes. David went down to wait by the dock while I sat with Lena and Bert on the patio. No bugs bit; there were no bugs. I confessed I had had a great fear of losing myself in the ayahuasca.

"Always that way," said Bert. "We're always afraid of losing what we know, afraid of dying. And it's a new life when we return."

David shouted from the dock. A boat was coming. The three of us ran the bags to the river. On the embankment I hugged Lena and Bert. A Coca Cola boat was coming in.

On the river David said, "At last I see you smile."

I looked at him. The boatman sat behind us in the noise of the motor, out of reach.

"It's the first time you've really smiled since we left Atalaya. I had no face for you there at the *fondo*. It was as if I didn't exist."

His eyes held no reproach. It was simply an observation. The sky behind him was silver with clouds. His thick black hair stood up in the wind. He was remarkably handsome. The desire to have a child returned. It was almost palpable; my whole body wanted it. It seemed the world around me did, too. The jungle was a constantly pregnant place. Any soul coming in on our lovemaking, immersed as it was in *madre selva,* would be an amazing child.

But getting pregnant? Not an easy task for a forty-three year old who smoked acres of tobacco and jumped into every new minute as though she had limitless time. Recently David had said I had the vagina of a fifteen year old. But it wasn't youth. It was sex in unlimited doses that brought the adolescent attributes of swollen lower lip and supple spine.

I smiled, and he grabbed my hand.

"Just look what will be lost to you once you are gone," he said, reading my mind.

The sky down river was turquoise green and clearing.

"I don't want to look ahead," I said. "It will make me lose the minutes I have and I don't want that."

He kissed me on the mouth, which surprised me. Then he put his arm around my shoulder, but I pulled away.

"It's not the world I'm afraid will see, not the Calle Ene —" I gestured around us at the empty water, "I'm just impatient with possessiveness. Does that make sense?"

He moved brusquely to the far end of the narrow seat. His eyes did not look angry but I couldn't be sure. Suddenly he hauled up his hand from the river and splashed me in the face. I was caught off-guard. It took me a minute to get him back. I wet his shirt. He got me again. We kept it up, back and forth, until we were both soaking wet. The boatman, coolly impassive next to the roaring motor, started to laugh. He had wonderful teeth.

It was almost dark when we docked in Atalaya. Mélida waved to us from her kiosk and called her husband to watch us come in. It was hard to say how old she was. Her youngest child was a three year old girl, who twirled and twirled in her little dresses, and was picked up and spoiled by everyone. Her grandchild by her eldest son was a girl the same age. Her husband seemed much younger than she was, but Mélida had the timeless face of a woman of the land.

No laughter trailed David and me as we walked the streets, short and tall together. No gossip paused as we passed by. But even if it had, I would have welcomed the steamy little town and our room off the courtyard of Don Simeon's. We went down to Mélida's to break our fast.

Her father was a vigorous looking man who might have been eighty. Hearing where we'd come from, he told of his own first time with ayahuasca. He'd taken it because of pains in his chest. A doctor had told him he had tuberculosis. Fearful, the old man had gone to a *curandero*. Within a week he was healthy again.

Mélida's eyes glittered in the candlelight.

"I took it for protection," she said. "It's true as they say, every sorcerer has an animal shape. At least one, sometimes many. If you can see that shape, you've penetrated a secret. Then he or she can have no control over you. Years ago, there was someone fighting me, trying to control me. I didn't know who it was. I went to a *curandero* I trusted because I needed to *see* my enemy's animal. I needed to protect myself."

She gestured to the street and the people walking.

"There are some, I can tell you, who want to do harm. They want to rule over your will. There are some in this town — three or four — and I see them. And they know I can see them. They don't dare try anything on me or my family.

"I went to the *curandero*, who recognized that I was under attack. I stayed with him. No salt, no grease, no meat, no sugar. For months I fasted, and traveled on the ayahuasca until I could see. When I came away from there, I could identify everyone's animal, and can to this day."

Her black hair shadowed her eyes as she looked at the river. "There's one around here — " Her voice rose as if she meant to be overheard,"—who is a black bird. A great malevolent black bird. He knows who I mean."

I didn't dare turn around. In my mind's eye a shadowy figure in the moonlight ducked behind a wall. Surfaces changed places. Reality shifted gears. The moon that had been bright and growing, lighting up the landscape as it sailed above the town, slid into a cloud.

After almost a week of rain, the weather cleared. We were making love when someone knocked on the door. The first plane had come in, and my name was on it. The next sure flight might not be for ten days. David jumped up, and I felt like something had been ripped away.

"Painful today, painful tomorrow. Does it matter when?"

I spoke as the door closed behind him. He went to see if my flight could be changed. Meanwhile, he told me to pack. Gathering my things, I calculated the days we'd been together since my last period. To be certain, we would need more time. I leaned against the wall.

He came back in, shaking his head. "There won't be another flight. You have to go now. Hurry, they're waiting."

Under the *mamei* tree at the airstrip, I was like someone used to speaking with a constant companion who is suddenly not there. On the plane I realized we would not have the full moon together—something I had taken for granted. The picture I carried was of him that morning underneath me—his dark eyes half closed, watching my face. It had already taken on the weight of an ikon as our plane approached the Andean wall.

I loved the whole country, the length and breadth of it— mountain, desert, and jungle—every inch. I loved the smell of soap in the airports, the soap people used to wash their clothes that always greeted me on my arrival. Even blindfolded I would know where I was. I loved all the possibilities denied, it seemed, in ordinary life. And I was leaving. The green mat with silver ribbons stretched out beneath us. I was going away.

I had been clear about telling David of my lover in Lima, my lover in America—leaving avenues of escape, of not belonging to him or to anyone. The irony was that I was guarding his face inside myself already, like a sacred image. I would bring it back, and dream of him in the dark. I'd done it before. By holding on to the way it had been, I stopped it from changing. All risk was gone. The jewel encrusted treasure would never hatch.

He was thinking of me, I could feel him. It was almost eleven in the morning. He had already gone down to Mélida's and told her about my departure, and taken his cup of black coffee. Now he was walking the streets in the hot sun, holding onto loss like an egg of his own.

I was sitting on the floor in Lima, surrounded by all the things I hadn't packed: toucan feathers, huayruru beads, woven bracelets, a handful of jungle herbs, and the tiger's tooth David had given me, the clay pot I'd traded for my penknife with the Chapibo woman in Pucallpa, some fabric painted in the serpent design, and some ripe guayabas.

The guayabas were half-riddled with worms—most likely maggots—strangely dormant in Lima's winter cold. I decided to eat them anyway. It would be the last bite I'd have before taking the plane to the U.S. I thought of my friend with the tour guide returning to the jungle with all the fruits of her life in her hands.

Perhaps she was already building her house. Perhaps she would conceive the baby I'd wanted and more than likely would never have. But the fruitfulness I celebrated, and that I'd forgotten existed, did not require a product or a reason. It was sensuality as normal ground, as base for a largeness, a wildness in myself. It occurred to the extent that I wanted to enjoy it, but did not properly belong to me.

My flight would leave in less than four hours. I would wake up the next day beyond the reach of Bolivar soap, beyond the possibility of a short hop back to the jungle. I thought back to my night with the ayahuasca, remembering how my shadow had detached itself from some trees, and attached to others. There was a sweet almost dispassionate quality in the shadow weaving through the leaves. Like the face of a mother with a wolfish grin, there was nothing personal in it. It simply moved.

Cordillera Blanca

"The Shining Path controls the roads. When they declare an armed strike on the highways, they mean it. Everything stops. Nobody travels."

I was standing with three friends on a side street in Barranco, Lima. I had just returned from America. It was drizzling as it often did in winter, a fine mist the Limeñans called *garua*.

"There's a good chance you could die out there."

My friends were Peruvian artists and intellectuals who rarely left the city. Their vision of the world was colored by the frequent blackouts in Lima caused by the guerrilla group Sendero Luminoso, the Shining Path; by the horrendous news on TV day after day, and through the grapevine of Radio Bemba, the radio of word of mouth, with people passing the news so fast at times it was astonishing.

Arriving from New York, I wanted to leave for the town of Huaraz in the Callejón de Huaylas, two hundred and fifty miles north of Lima. *Callejón* means alley. The narrow valley of Huaylas stretched north to south for a hundred and ten miles between two mountain ranges, Cordillera Blanca and Cordillera Negra, white and black, named for the color of their peaks.

The Humboldt current brought cold wet air from the ocean which passed over the low bare peaks of the Black Range and settled farther east in the White Range in the form of glaciers. I'd been coming to the South American mountains for almost twenty years. I'd lived in Cuzco and on Lake Titicaca, and had traveled through much of the Andes, but this was the first time I was aiming to spend weeks trekking among them.

I had spent the past two years—after giving up smoking—climbing every peak in the Catskills, first in summer, then in winter. The hardships I'd encountered and overcome gave me new confidence and enthusiasm as a hiker. Now I was hoping to know firsthand the mountains I had always seen from a distance. I was hoping the intimacy with a land mass I had loved for so long would reveal something more than it already had.

"This isn't like years ago," one friend insisted. "it isn't safe now to walk, especially if you're a gringa."

That night I called another friend, a lawyer who was also a hunter. He had covered much of Peru on foot or by jeep. From the heads and horns and rugs I'd seen adorning his house, I'd gathered he was a good shot.

"Pepe," I said, "I want to hike the Cordillera Blanca. Is it as dangerous as they say?"

He laughed. "Maybe not. But there are some things to remember. The Callejón de Huaylas is still relatively safe. The people have enough food and work; they don't want the Shining Path coming in and telling them what to do. But the other valley, Callejón de Canchucos, is another story. It's close to the jungle, where Sendero can duck for cover. If you walk that way, avoid the town of Yanama. It's where the army found all those guns. And under no conditions should you go alone. I know a guide. My friend is godfather to his son. Eusebio Atusparia. He works as a carpenter in the hospital of Huaraz. Tell him I sent you."

Pepe laughed again. "And don't let his humble demeanor fool you. He is one of Peru's great mountain climbers."

Since most of the assaults on the buses happened at night, I bought a ticket for the seven a.m. to Huaraz. Arriving at three in the afternoon, I went straight to the hospital.

Eusebio Atusparia looked to be a man in his forties, with the hooked nose and sharply defined cheekbones of the native mountain people. The recent absence of European and American alpinists had reduced his work, so he was glad to hear of the trek. The price he quoted included himself as guide and cook, the burro who would carry our goods with the mule driver and his son.

Three days later we arrived by jeep at the tiny village of Cashapampa, the start of our trek at 9,500 feet, where Juan the mule driver lived with his family. The importance of Cashapampa lay in its position at the base of Quebrada de Santa Cruz, one of the main arteries connecting Callejón de Huaylas with Callejón de Canchucos to the east.

Quebrada means gorge or ravine, and comes from *quebrar,* to break. A *quebrada* was where the land broke sharply into steep defiles. Our whole journey would consist of climbing up one long *quebrada,* over the pass between two peaks and down the other side; then around and up again over the next pass, and so forth—threading the Cordillera Blanca through some of Peru's highest mountains.

We piled our goods onto Juan's patio and watched the activity around us. Juan was having a birthday party for his brother, who had come in from Chimbotes, and we were invited. I received the news with mixed feelings. Though not the highest mountains in the world, the Andes rose precipitously from the valley floor; the abrupt change in altitude at the onset would require considerable stamina. The first day of a trek was always the hardest for me. It would only be complicated by drinking, staying up late, and leaving, more than likely, with a hangover in the morning.

Of course, it wasn't as though I had a choice. The children showed me the way to the river where I could wash. When I got back it was almost dark. Juan's house was built on the edge of a steep hill. His roof extended out over the patio where we would sleep. Wooden stairs descended to the main room and the kitchen, then down again to the stalls of the animals. Since I had declined the invitation of roast pig, Eusebio had made some tuna sandwiches, then disappeared into the house below.

It was only 6:30 but the cold night was already folding in. The southern constellations dotted the darkness and I moved to get a better view. Alpha Centaurus and the Southern Cross; Ara the altar; Fomalhaut in the southern fish, Piscis Austrinis; and just off the tail of Scorpio, a near perfect half heart of equidistant stars called Corona Australis. I welcomed them like old friends.

The musicians had already arrived and were tuning up. A constant stream of people passed the patio and descended the stairs. From the smell of roast pork and clatter of tin plates, I imagined the banquet: grandmothers in their shawls and bowler hats nodded in time to the music. The half heart I'd been watching in the sky seemed to fill up with harps, drums, and people dancing. I made my way down the stairs.

A rush of warm air hit me at the door. In the cave-like room Eusebio waved me over to a seat beside him at the table. The musicians in the corner, half hidden in the darkness and the shadow of their hat brims, were playing a *huayno,* a fast dancing tune. There were two violins, a harp, a *quena,* the Andean bamboo flute, and a drum. A teenage boy joined the musicians with his *huyro,* a scored cylindrical gourd. Rubbed with a stick, the gourd made a sound like a cicada.

Juan gave me a glass of *cañaso,* the homemade cane liquor. A baby crawled in the dust under the table. An agile young man jumped into the middle of the floor and began to strut backwards and forwards, gleeful with his own grace and power as a cock in the barnyard. Around him the men and women danced and stamped, raising swirls of dust in the light from the kerosene lantern. Against the wall a line of young boys watched everything with rapt attention. I was glad I'd been invited. Juan came by and filled my glass again.

Around ten, I made my way to the door and up the stairs. Compared to the party the patio was cold and deserted. The Scorpion and Altar had set in the west. Though I plugged my ears and pulled my sleeping bag over my head, the drum came through the floor and into my dreams.

I awoke to a rustling noise beside me: Eusebio was rolling out his bag. Below, the party was going strong.

"I thought you would stay much later," I said.

He shook his head. "Some men are passing out leaflets and talking in the corners. Propaganda. I don't know them. They are not from around here. I prefer not to get involved."

"Does Juan know them?"

"No, but it's his house. He can't refuse them entry to his party."

"Do you think it's—"

Eusebio put his finger to his mouth and I stopped speaking.

The townspeople gathered about Juan and Eusebio loading the burro. Most of them looked like they hadn't slept all night. Under the tugging and pulling, the burro wore the sweet patient expression of his race. Juan's son, Marc Antonio, said the burro was called Alfonso after his owner, which struck me as a happy coincidence. The burro had the same profile as Alfonsín, the president of Argentina.

It was eleven by the time we set out. Barely half a kilometer up the trail Juan announced he would have to turn back. He had sharp pains in his stomach, he said, and would have to lie down. It seemed obvious to me he wanted to return to his party. I looked at Eusebio, who said nothing.

Juan said his nephew, who'd been walking with us, would work in his stead. The boy was around thirteen, the same age as Marc Antonio, and looked capable enough, but none of this boded well with me. Would Juan catch up with us as he said? How could he unless he traveled in the dark?

The uphill climb was hot, dry, steep, and relentless. I was right about the liquor robbing my energy. None of my companions' cheer rubbed off. After two hours, their insistence that our campsite was *aquí no más, aquicito no más*—very close, right here—made me want to scream. Even without a pack my heart was racing, and my legs were heavy. I knew we were nowhere near the end of the day's trek.

To escape the sun and let my heart catch up, I heaved myself under a ledge into a small spot of shadow. I didn't see the thorn bush until too late. I sat right on it and lost control. I yelled about the hill, the awful night before, my lack of sleep. It was either cry or scream. Didn't they see my lack of acclimation? My need for water, for air? Running out of things to attack, I lapsed into scowling silence.

Eusebio suggested calmly that if I were unable to go on, we simply turn back. I fell into step behind the slow and constant Alfonso, feeling much like a recalcitrant burro myself. Since I had chosen the ascent of Calvary, I hoped at least I was expiating some sins. Trudging along with my head down, I studied the ground, the rocks and pebbles, the dusty plants.

I bumped into Eusebio. He and Juan's nephew stood smack in the middle of the path. I looked up. On either side of us were two men, unshaven and angry looking. Alfonso and Marc Antonio were up ahead. One man stood on the edge of the drop, looking down the valley as though waiting for someone. Since most people in the mountains offered some kind of greeting, the silence made me uneasy.

"Where are you going?" the one on the edge demanded.

I thought, They're not mountain people. They're bandits or Sendero. Eusebio and the boys are no match for them. They didn't look like they were carrying guns. On the other hand, a very slim knife could slit all our throats. The man on the edge caught me studying him and I cast my eyes down. I had the wrong color hair to attempt any confrontation of wills.

"We're up here to do some fishing," said Eusebio. "Our friends from the village are coming up shortly." He sounded calm and self-possessed.

The speaker jutted his chin toward Marc Antonio, watching us from up the trail. "The boy says you're headed for the pass, and down the other side to Colcabamba, near Yanama."

"That's what he would like to do, but we're going fishing, *aquicito no más,* right up ahead."

"Not staying overnight?"

Eusebio shook his head. "Our friends are coming up from

Cashapampa. We'll walk down together in the dark."

The man waved us on like an imperious border guard. Eusebio raised his hand in salute. I watched peripherally, looking everywhere but at their faces. I could feel their eyes on us until we rounded the curve and were lost to view.

Marc Antonio had waited. We walked together for a good fifteen minutes without speaking. When Eusebio stopped, he looked at the trail behind us, then at the boy.

"Do you know them?"

Marc Antonio shook his head. "They're not from around here. They asked where we were going, so I told them. I never thought—"

"This is a good lesson," Eusebio said, looking at the three of us. "If you don't know them, don't tell the truth. They might want to hurt you. There are too many dangerous people in the mountains these days."

"Do you think they'll follow us?" I said. "I mean, kill us in our tents tonight?"

"They could have done that already if they'd wanted to. They're here for something else, I think, and don't want to be bothered. This is a well-traveled route. We'd be found soon enough, and they don't want trouble. They will check where we are staying tonight. That I'm sure of. And Juan will come just in time."

We reached level ground in the widening *quebrada,* near the banks of a fast moving river. It was five in the afternoon; Eusebio said we would make camp. I went directly to the giant boulders at the river bank. I washed behind them in the freezing water while I was still hot.

The water returned me to myself. I put on clean clothes, washed out the dirty ones, and calmly considered that if we were going to be murdered we would be, and there was nothing I could do about it. I trusted Eusebio's judgement. As for my recent outburst, I was simply out of shape and needed to be more patient with myself and my companions.

I came back to two tents set up by a roaring fire. The boys had caught a few fish to add to dinner. Night came in quickly. I ate, watching the sparks fly up into the sky. Evidently we were not trying to hide our presence. Alfonso stood motionless on the other side of the fire. His eyes reflecting the flames glittered red and yellow in the dark.

Opening the tent Eusebio said was mine, I found two sleeping bags laid out. I considered this interesting turn of events and looked at him. He said he would wait for me to get ready before coming in. King Solomon might have said the same thing to one of his wives, but I was sure that was not what he meant.

I tried both sleeping places, chose one, and arranged my things beside it. I stuck a candle to a flat rock and placed it at the bottom of the tent. I lit up the sage and sweet grass I'd brought and blew the smoke to the four directions.

Laying the smoking bundle beside the candle, I surveyed my rustic altar and blew out the flame. I plugged my ears and pulled the sleeping bag over my head. When Eusebio entered he crawled in his bag, zipped it up, and went to sleep quickly. As I expected, he snored.

Vacating the tent was my only job in the morning. They struck the tents and packed the burro while I did yoga by the river. I noticed Juan had not returned and that nobody was mentioning it. Eusebio showed me where we were on the map, and the distance we would want to cover by the evening's camp. Unlike the day before, he said, it would be easy walking.

As we headed east, the glacier Taulliraju appeared at the far end, watching over the valley. Almost all the place names in the Peruvian Andes are in Quechua. *Raju* means ice. *Taulli* was the name for the cornflower-blue lupine that grew in such profusion in the dips and hollows of the ground we covered, and across the hillsides. It made me smile to think the mountain took its name from the flowers growing on its flanks, and not the other way around.

The land was much more level and we kept up a good pace,

accompanied by the rollicking Taullimayo river that paralleled the trail. *Mayo* means river, and this one was also named for the lupine. The rocky defile widened out. Behind us, the deep V of the cleft against the sky receded as we entered the abode of the mountains. This was their territory, their domain.

After masses of flowering female lupine, we reached a plateau of only male plants, like an army of purple candles. The stamen of each plant stuck three feet up from the leaves and was covered with tiny purple flowers. The new young plants had a stamen of whitish unopened flowers, and a soft cobwebby skin to the touch, like velvet.

At a small green lake Eusebio pointed out the glaciers Santa Cruz, Pumapampa, and Nevado Caraz. I caught the joy and ownership in his voice as he named their elevation and showed us the way he had scaled them. I was just a hiker, but I held a keen delight in any land I covered. Like Thoreau, I felt every landscape I had ever walked belonged to me.

Juan surprised us coming down the trail at a rapid pace. He had left his house at twilight, he said, and walked all night. We were not at the campsite where he'd expected to find us, but on the road he'd met a mule driver who had passed our camp and told him where we were. Juan had not seen the two men who'd stopped us.

Juan sent his nephew back and Marc Antonio offered to accompany his cousin part of the way down. I loved how they could nonchalantly cover such distance and thousands of feet of altitude differential in just the way I might offer to take a friend to the wild leek fields behind my house. The difference was in degree.

The next day we would go over the first pass, and I was looking ahead with trepidation. Some days I had atrial fibrillation. Instead of beating steadily, my heart fluttered. Not enough blood got pumped through my body. It left me debilitated. The doctors had counseled rest when it occurred, but that would not be an option on the trail.

For two years in the United States I had been studying shaman-ism, and practicing a technique called journeying, wherein one travels blindfolded to the sound of a beaten drum. One either goes to the lower world where the animal allies live, or the upper world to meet one's teacher. Arguments could be made that these enti-ties one perceived were really farflung reaches of one's own psy-che. Whatever the source, I'd found the knowledge imparted from both the animals and the teacher to be useful, and the feeling of protection undeniable.

Before leaving for Peru, I had asked about climbing the Andes with my heart condition. The answer was unequivocal: Flow, don't push. There is nowhere you can't go. Flow, don't push. Respect and honor the body, and you are protected.

Meanwhile, I had brought along Coramine—a respiratory stimulant for high altitudes—ginseng, electrolytes, vitamins, and coca leaves. The way the native people walked the Andes was to measure the distance in mouthfuls of coca— how many mouth-fuls one chewed to reach the top. The only thing I did not have was the *llycllya,* the splinter of limestone to chew with the leaves. Mixed with saliva, it precipitated the alkaloid out of the leaf.

As the landscape grew more barren, the flowers seemed more wildly beautiful. Each one came as an unexpected gift. Eusebio knew them all: the multi-colored daisy, called Butterfly of a Thousand Colors and the yellow daisy, Butterfly of the Ground. The tiny white five petaled flower, tapush'ka, was supposed to close up when you spoke its name up close. *Tapush'ka?* The word in Quechua meant "to ask."

The mountain bowl widened out to an amphitheater. Halfway in was a lone house with extensive corrals. At the door an old man with green teeth greeted us warmly. Seeing he was a *chaq'chero,* a per-son who chewed coca, I asked if he had any *llyclla* he could spare for crossing the pass. He smiled broadly and handed me a lump of dark stone from his pocket. We gave him some fresh oranges in return.

Around a bend in the amphitheater was a large green lake. A

yellow bird flying above it caught my eye. Eusebio said it was the ácaca, named for its call—ácaca ácaca brrrrr—like laughter as it swooped above us. The ácaca lived only above 12,000 feet and made its nest by pecking out a hole with its ivory colored beak in the solid rock. One legend said that the bird had taught the Inca which herb to use to soften the stone, and helped them fling up their fortresses with ease. It was a beige colored bird with a clean contour that blended in with the rocks, except when it flew and revealed the yellow vest it wore under its wings.

At the upper reaches of the lake the river rejoined us, and my energies were beginning to flag. The *kenhual* trees, native trees with red papery bark, cast deep pools of shadow in the late afternoon sun. Eusebio pointed out a mountain in the perfect shape of a pyramid to our left. Alpamayo had been voted the most beautiful mountain in the world by a congress of mountain climbers in Munich 1955, he said. All I wanted to do was sit down.

We passed through a narrow waist of rock to a smaller bowl; at its upper reaches was a grove of *kishuar* trees, another native tree with small thorny looking leaves. Kishuar k'uta the place was called: little corner of kishuar trees, —our new campsite. I didn't care what it was called. By my reckonings we had walked fourteen kilometers and climbed almost two thousand feet.

I pulled my pack off Alfonso, grabbed my towel and clean clothes and went off to wash. Hidden from view at the river, I stripped to the waist and rinsed the sweat off the top half of my body. The sun was going down. I put on a clean shirt, stripped from the waist down, and entered the river. The water was freezing. I washed in a flash and jumped out. My teeth were chattering. Once I had clothes on I could relax.

I threw my sweaty clothes into the water and washed them one by one. Beside me a taulli bush laden with female flowers rocked in the wind. Pulling some branches together, I put my face into the blue-purple bouquet. They had a deep musty smell. I picked one flower and put it in the band of my hat.

The river hurtled over rounded rocks in the narrow channel, down the steep incline. Kneeling over, I laid my ear against the grassy bank and caught the full impact of the basso profundo gurgling drone. It was the same river we'd been walking with all day. The river of lupine. My fingers were tingling with the cold. The love I felt came from my stomach. I belonged to that old river.

In the dawn light the glaciers around me were stern forbidding presences—a fitting backdrop to the stony uphill valley floor. While the men loaded Alfonso I hopped up the trail, saying I wanted to scout out the trek. Punta Unión stood at 4800 meters, only 700 meters up from our campsite, roughly 2300 feet. I'd done climbs like that through pleasant Catskill mountain afternoons, but not at that altitude. In fact, I was not so much scouting the land as asking permission to pass over it safely to the other side.

Years before, on my first visit to the Andes, I'd learned that mountains were not metaphors for wilderness, but entities in themselves. Walking above Cuzco, I'd met an old man who spoke some Spanish. I'd pointed to a dazzling snow-capped mountain and asked its name.

"Apu Auzangate," he said.

"And that one?" I pointed to another.

"Apu Salkantay."

"*Apu* means mountain?"

He squinted at Salkantay, and held up his hand in salute.

"It means the god in that place: Salkantay'."

At the head of the valley was the craggy peak whose shoulder formed one half of the pass we aimed to cross: Apu Taulliraju. I saluted like the old man had and hoped for the best.

I carried almost nothing. In my day pack was only water, a journal, a camera and a sweater; but even they grew heavier as we advanced. I started taking low angle shots so I could throw myself on the ground and rest. I shot a whole roll of film, apparently taking careful aim at what turned out to be ordinary rocks, my feet, and the puna grass around me.

My pace became extraordinarily slow, like that of a grand-mother burro out for her last trek in the sun. In fact, the ridge line we climbed was called Mal Paso, wrong step, because of the precipitous drop and the quantity of burros that had slipped and fallen. Their bleached skulls vied with Taulliraju's glacier for whiteness.

Of all the aids I'd brought to help me, what worked best was not coca leaves or electrolytes, but dogged determination. There was no pride in it. It was not the pace of heroes. With my heart pounding wildly in the diminishing oxygen, there was not even the hope of reaching the top. There was no top, only one more turn up the trail. Only fifteen minutes more. One more mouthful of water. *Aquicito no más.* You are almost there.

The pass came as a shock. Two rock walls and a space between them that opened onto an immense valley. The Callejón de Canchucos. Two men and a woman were leaning against the walls, looking out. Eusebio, Juan, Marc Antonio and Alfonso joined them. I threw myself on the ground where I stood. I looked at the distance we had covered, immensely grateful for every inch that I'd made.

Taking pictures by the slab sides of the pass, I found a shyness I had not expected in Marc Antonio. When I gave him the camera to take his turn our hands touched. He jumped back slightly and looked down. Because he was small and our interaction had been so slight, I had been thinking of him as a child. But standing before me was a young man.

I tapped his shoulder playfully. "I hope with these faces the camera won't break."

When I joined the group to face him, he was smiling.

Eusebio insisted we get moving again. He pointed to the sun. We had a long way to our next campsite and not much time. As far as I was concerned, we were heroes. We had made the pass. Why drive ourselves to accomplish more? He replied it was purely practical. We needed to sleep, and the lower down we did it, the better.

Every cartilage in my knees and every bone in my feet complained at the forced march down the rocky slope. I became the trail sweeper, getting farther and farther behind as the afternoon wore on. At a bend in the road they stopped and waited.

When I caught up, Eusebio handed me a fleshy rose-like flower on a stubby stem. Its flamboyance was in such wild contrast to the grim land around us. The yellow center turned by degrees into bright red on the outer petals. The stout hardy flower was called Rima Rima. Eusebio said it only grew above 14,000 feet. I put it in the band of my hat.

We made camp at a fork in the road that led to another pass between Taulliraju and the glacier Pucaraju. Our campsite was still too high to provide any pasturage for Alfonso, but I could go no farther. Juan grumbled as he set out in search of food for the burro.

The spring I found to wash in was a muddy crease where two slopes converged. I sank in up to my ankles and struggled to wash without dropping anything in the black ooze. Our dinner was a thrown together affair of boiled chicken and gummy noodles. Threatening clouds moved in and piled above us. We had barely finished eating when it started to hail.

In the tent I listened to Eusebio snore. How strange it was to sleep in such an intimate space with someone I was not making love with. He was becoming more attractive to me the more time we spent together. He walked and packed and cooked and did everything with an economy of movement I found admirable. And his knowledge of the mountains seemed inexhaustible.

I tried to find a tolerable position on the stony ground. The difference between comfortable repose and restless restraint, I decided, was freedom of choice. Within the confines of a shared tent I couldn't move freely. What would I say if I woke him up—that we should make love? Then again, why not? The attraction I felt was not just from my side. And if I didn't speak, I knew he wouldn't.

The first thing I noticed, poking my head through the tent flap, was Juan's feet in black rubber sandals walking through slush that had piled up from the night before. They looked red and cold. Everyone was moving with alacrity, preparing for a quick departure, and I jumped out to help. No one faulted me for their having to spend a wretched night so close to the pass, but I felt guilty anyway.

We were headed down the long slopes south and eastward, out from the shadow of the mountains toward the wide valley of Canchucos. We passed a caravan of twenty burros and eight German trekkers, along with their cooks, guides, and helpers. They had come down from Portachuelo de Llanganuco, the popular pass above Llanganuco Lake, which we would by-pass on our way to Quebrada Ulta, one valley beyond. I suddenly felt proud of my one modest pack riding atop Alfonso with our gear.

By mid-afternoon we were in Colcabamba, a village nestled among slopes jammed precipitously together, and cut through by a river. Down the valley to the east was the town of Yanama, the Shining Path stronghold my friend in Lima had cautioned me to avoid. We made camp fifty yards from the town square.

Across the valley came the wild insistent tonal scale of an Andean bamboo flute accompanied by several large drums. In a field on the far slope some men were leading horses around and around in time to the music while other men were dancing. Eusebio explained it was the Festival of Wheat.

Though most people owned their own plots of land, all heavy work was done communally. The men we watched were cutting down wheat and heaping it up. They led the horses over the pile and danced and stamped on it themselves to separate the wheat from the chaff. When the sun-bleached piles were pitched in the air, the wind carried away the chaff and the kernels fell to the ground. The owner of the field had brought the musicians and cane liquor, and when it was the next man's turn for his field, he would do the same.

Colcabamba had three roads out: the one we'd come in on, the trail up to Llanganuco, and the road down Canchucos valley to the town of Yanama near the jungle, where Sendero could slip in and out unnoticed. Halfway between us and Yanama was the village of Potaca. One fork led up from there to Quebrada Ulta, where we were going.

I visited the hotel in the town square. A middle-aged woman, with strands of gray hair mixed into her long black braids, invited me in to sign her guest book.

"Are you German?" she asked.

"No, American."

"Ah," she said, looking at the name I'd printed. "The other woman was American also. She signed in here and stayed the night. The next day she disappeared."

"Disappeared?"

"They never found her or her things or her body. She was heading for Llanganuco, but she never arrived."

I had learned in my dealings with people to not mention Sendero by name unless they did.

"Then the two young Englishmen were chased by men with guns," she continued. "One was shot, but the other ran back here for help. By the time he returned with men from our village, his friend was dead."

"It's certainly better not to travel alone," I said. "I always used to, but in these times, I wouldn't consider it."

She nodded. "In these times it's better not to."

In the evening I invited Eusebio for a beer in the hotel owner's kitchen. As night closed in, the woman's brother dropped in with one of her neighbors. The woman was a widow and did not like being alone at night. She served Eusebio and me at the kitchen table.

"Why won't they leave us alone?" she said aloud in the cave-like room to no one in particular. "They want to tell us how to live, what to plant, and what we can own. These are decisions for the community to make, not outsiders."

I thought of her position. She'd been left property by her husband and ran her own hotel, however sporadically; she was Colcabamba's version of a middle class woman. The Shining Path directed its efforts to better the lives of the farmers, the *campesinos;* to take from the rich and middle class and redistribute land and property among the poor; to establish a socialist order which they would lead. They would always be this woman's enemy.

"Mo matter what decision we make," said the brother, "Sendero always knows. Someone in our town is telling them."

"Someone in every town," said the neighbor.

The beer made me slightly tipsy. As Eusebio and I walked back to the tents, I decided there was nothing wrong in feeling desire. I decided it was now or never. Once he entered the tent and got in his bag, I asked if he didn't find it a little strange sleeping with a woman night after night in the tiny space we had, without making love.

He was quiet a moment. Finally he said no.

"Have you ever done this before?"

"Yes. A mountain climber came here every year until she made it to the top of Huascarán. It took her three tries, but she made it."

"And you weren't lovers?"

"The only woman I've ever made love to is my wife."

I was nonplused. Whether it was true or not was not the point. Clearly he did not need to act out the attraction he felt by making love. I turned to answer him but he was already snoring.

Instead of going all the way down to the fork at Potaca, we zigzagged upward, going over the slopes of the hills in a technique they called *faldeando,* skirting. The seemingly erratic amble was actually cutting a line, like the hypotenuse of a triangle, to the path up Quebrada Ulta.

One hour up gave us a splendid view of the wide lush valley of Canchucos spread out below. Except for the dip in an intervening valley, gaining the path and ascending it lasted all day. Keeping my eyes on the ground, I contemplated the rules I was learning on the uphill climb:

1) Never make the road longer or harder than it is. *Aquicito no más* is a good philosophy.

2) Make much of every bright or beautiful thing that crosses your eye or enters your mind.

3) Acceptance of the uphill climb as a necessity in reaching the top leads not to submission, but a sense of calm, and a readiness to accept whatever happens.

4) Acceptance of oneself in strength and weakness goes a long way in saving energy. Agitation uses up a third of expendable energy; more if directed against oneself.

5) Make much of the view from any rest stop. After the long march of stones on the ground, the opening out over distance is a benediction, and deserves your gratitude.

6) Putting forth your best effort relieves the ego of its need to justify its existence. The strenuous push is equalled by internal effort. The uphill climb, like orgasm, leaves little energy remaining but to cry, laugh, or love everything without hesitation.

Marc Antonio came up behind me, and patted my shoulder.

"Half as many rest stops as the last climb." He nodded approvingly, "You're gaining strength."

I smiled in response.

At three thirty in the afternoon, we reached a flat place on the barren slope that would be our campsite for the night. We had gained 4,600 feet since the morning and reached 14,400 feet. I rushed to wash while I was still hot.

Avalanches sounded from the glacier Chopicalqui, reclining like a sphinx against the sky. I threw my washcloth into the icy stream that was reflecting the red gold afternoon sun. The water kept up a trickling sound over the flat rocks until it reached the rim of the bowl, where it dropped down to the valley far below. I pulled off my clothes and surveyed my bathtub. Surrounded by glaciers, the water rippled in a steady breeze at the edge of the world.

How like the water was my own sensuality, renewed from within, sexual from the inside out. I liked standing naked under the sky in the very last minutes of hot sun. I liked leaning over, letting the water slide over my skin and carry away the sweat. I liked that my own desire spilled over the edges of myself and came forward without hesitation. I loved being a woman. An ácaca bird cried out from the nearby slope: once, twice, then set up her trill. I smiled as the river dropped off the edge. My power was that I also could flow—with wild abandon if I chose. Like the river that was my song.

I came back to the campsite. Venus flickered through the smoke of the campfire. At the entrance to the tent were three Rima Rima flowers tied together with a strand of puna grass. I looked at the backs of the two men and the boy, busy about the fire and the meal. Inside the tent all my things had been placed next to a single mat and sleeping bag.

The clear night gave way to menacing clouds at dawn. By the time we were packed it had started to snow. I insisted Juan and Marc Antonio take my extra socks and wear them inside plastic bags in their rubber sandals. The great V behind us, formed by the slopes on either side, became dwarfed under clouds as we trudged ahead.

We made it to an overhanging ledge and stepped inside to rest. Alfonso found a clump of puna grass and browsed unconcerned as the snow on his coat melted. To the northwest the clouds had lifted, revealing two glaciers, Yanapaccha and Pisco, the same name as the Peruvian liquor made from sugar cane.

Eusebio pointed to Pisco. "If you worked as hard as you are working now, you could scale that glacier in five days."

"Really?"

"You would have to train for a pair of weeks, climb up and down as we're doing now. Then you'd be prepared for the altitude. Look," he pointed, "you would enter from the bowl of Llanganuco above the lakes. Then you would gain the col between Huandoy and Pisco, about 5,200 meters. It would take two camp sites up the slope to get the top, at 5,800 meters."

"You really think I could do it? My heart has a hard time in these heights."

He looked at me appraisingly. "But you have a will, which is half the battle. And Pisco is the easiest of them all. If you trained, I guarantee you could do it. The trick is to sleep low and climb high."

His finger moved up from the bowl of Llanganuco.

"You'd take two days to the col, and sleep there." He pointed halfway up the slope from the saddle, "That would be your last camp site. We'd start out at two in the morning and get the peak before noon, weather permitting. Then we'd walk back through our last campsite, sleep the night in the col again, and then out."

His face was animated as he spoke, and I could see he was on the slope he was describing, just as he was every time he pointed to a peak he'd climbed, explaining the best entry, the campsites, and the final ascent. As a guide he was enjoying our trek, but he was a climber first and foremost. He had scaled every glacier in the Cordillera Blanca, sometimes as the first Peruvian to do so. His enthusiasm was contagious.

None of us ate very much. I shared my apple with Alfonso. I was sorry I'd even mentioned my heart. As soon as we set out, it started clanging in my eardrums with a spastic cadence that made me weak and nervous. My breathing became difficult. Juan was afraid for Alfonso crossing the pass in the snow; he pulled ahead at a pace that left me farther and farther back. Flow, don't push, I reminded myself. Respect and honor the body, and there is nowhere you can't go.

I noticed the prints of some kind of dog in the snow. He must have passed recently; the tracks were still fresh. Were they fox? What was he doing up this high? They were definitely canine. The fox was the animal ally I usually met when I practiced journeying. I slowed to a steady more comfortable pace. Alfonso and my friends were lost to view.

I focused on tiny holes I passed in the wet snow—animal holes that went into the ground. In the journeying I'd learned to do you pictured yourself going down a hole, a real hole you knew of in the earth. That became your entrance to the lower world where the animal spirits lived. Once in their kingdom you followed their lead.

I concentrated on the snow. At the next hole, I hopped in and ran down a long stone corridor until I reached a cave. I found the fox and we ran together side by side between thick green hedges. The land beneath us changed to a cold stony plain that stretched for miles.

I looked at my prints in the snow and imagined the fox prints alongside, and how we would amble over to slopes we could not see, and keep running and running. The sparks flying from his fur, we flew over moony landscapes while I inched my way up the switchback. A boulder seemed to detach itself from the slope above me. It looked like the dark vigilant head of a giant turtle.

The earth and sky were a lithograph of grey, black and white. My friends cheered as I rounded the bend and came into view. Eusebio stayed behind, pacing me, as the father and son forged ahead with the burro. The fox danced around me with unflagging energy and irrepressible humor.

Dark slabs flanked the pass to a bleak sky. That was it. Portachuelo de Yanama. Thirteen hundred feet higher than the last pass. We'd made it.

> Where have all the colors gone to
> today, that is so black and white?

I pulled a plastic bag from my pocket and slowly smoothed it out on the wet ground. Sitting down, I burst into tears. I cradled my head on my arms and wept. No one moved to help me or asked why I was crying.

"*Soroche*," said Juan, matter-of-factly, altitude sickness.

I sobbed openly and without shame. I was released. No more uphill climb. Behind us, Canchucos was wide, green and brown. Before us, the bowl of grim gray mountains formed the headlands of the long Ulta valley sprawling westward.

We would camp in the bowl that night, Eusebio said. In the morning we'd go over the other Ulta pass, and back to the heights above Canchucos valley. From there we would skirt the *cerros,* the hills, up to the last pass, Portachuelo de Honda, then head down to Callejón de Huaylas where we'd started.

All I knew was that my heart was a church, and all the love I had for those mountains burned like candles at the altar. I watched as the wind swept the clouds into separate armies of rain that moved among the peaks. The sun burned through, illuminating the slopes on all sides. The sky took on a fresh washed blue as we made our way down through the slush.

The melting snow ran in rivulets down all vertical surfaces as the sun moved in and out of the clouds. Everything was dripping. In my black rain poncho, I felt I'd been walking among those peaks at a contemplative pace, dressed just as I was, for thousands of years. I studied the glaciers; the Andean summer had brought deep rifts and fissures that looked like black sticks laid across the whiteness.

Flow, don't push, said the rivulets and dripping rocks. Flow, don't push, said the fox behind me. The murmur of trickling water was broken from time to time by an avalanche in the distance. I realized I loved to walk among the peaks, not on them. I didn't want to scale them, bag them, take them, or penetrate their silence. I wanted only to walk among them, and love them close at hand.

My heart understood the mountains without me getting in the way. It was the land that shaped how I learned and what I gathered. A pilgrimage required effort; the effort served to remove obstruction. Then the place spoke in its own language directly to the heart. At the top of the world I had stepped out of time and was allowed or had allowed myself to love and be loved, unconditionally and without reserve.

We passed the fork we would take to scale the second Ulta pass the next day.

"Why are we going down?" I protested. "Won't we have to climb up again tomorrow?"

"Sleep low and climb high," said Eusebio. "We won't be worth anything tomorrow if we can't sleep tonight."

We made camp inside a rubble of stones that had once been the hut for some workmen. They had built it during the months they had worked on the pass we would cross the next day. A tunnel through solid rock. My head was clanging as I lay down. I thought of the effort it must have taken to move these stones to create the shelter. Just thinking about it made me tired.

The morning dawned iron cold and snowing slightly. I ventured out the door to a light dusting on the ground. Juan pointed down the mountain to where the path ducked out of view. "Can you see him?" he asked. "I can't figure out why he came up this far, so close to the pass, and went back. It doesn't make sense."

He pointed out barely visible tracks in the snow. One set came past our hut and up the trail, the other set went down. A person and a burro. I strained to see what he was pointing to. I'd realized when we'd first started the trek that no matter how I squinted, I would never see as well as my companions, who had gazed into far distances all their lives.

"There he is," Juan insisted, angling his arm to my line of vision. "Don't you see him?"

I did see something. There was a tiny speck of color moving. Whoever it was had a blue cap on. The rest of him and his burro blended in with the rocks.

"Maybe he was checking on us," I said. "Why didn't he greet us as he came through?"

Juan shrugged. "He passed while we were sleeping."

If not Sendero, maybe a thief, I thought. But that didn't make sense. When Eusebio returned, the three of them spoke in Quechua. Juan was a simple and observant man whose world rarely surprised him. Faced with the unexplainable he was like a dog with a flea: he worried it until it stopped or died.

At the fork above the hut I gave up my day pack to Alfonso for easier going. We labored up the bleak trail without speaking. The snow was replaced by a raw wind that nipped at our faces. I looked at the stoic burro, and not for the first time admired how he kept on going, no matter what.

Turning the bend, we came smack up against a wall of black boulders piled helter skelter, and the clear smell of sulphur in the air.

"Landslide," said Eusebio.

I looked up at the skyline. There was no pass, only a menacing conglomerate of loose rock inside a vertical bowl. I had a sudden vision of white snow dotted with drops of fresh blood, as if someone had just died. I wanted to leave immediately but Eusebio hopped up on one of the boulders.

While we watched, he picked his way upward like a human fly to see if there was a way over. I sat on a rock, my heart thumping. Above us the tiny silhouettes of two people came into view against the sky.

"Come this way," they shouted, pointing to the right. "You can make it from this side easy!"

Easy for them to say, I thought, they're not down here.

Eusebio shook his head. "No rope," he shouted, "and there's the burro." I was glad he didn't mention me.

"Like our friend, the blue hat, with *his* burro," Juan said, satisfied.

Eusebio took the map out of his pocket. There was no way over the pass; we would have to go down the Ulta ravine to where it opened onto Callejón de Huaylas. Then we'd be halfway between our starting point and the Honda valley, our original destination. We could walk out and catch a truck back to Huaraz, or we could skirt the *cerros* on the Huaylas side. We would reach the Honda valley above the town of Vicos, and follow the ravine up to the mountains on the other side of this landslide.

But we'd miss the pass. The thread we had planned to make through the length of the cordillera had been broken through no fault of our own. Skirting the hills through unfrequented lands might prove a lot more strenuous than the trail, but might also yield more wild life. I opted to go on.

His face lit up. "Of course, I know how sad you will be that we won't go over the pass to reach the last valley."

"Oh, devastated," I said.

I pulled my day pack off Alfonso and we headed down at a brisk pace. The sullen sky lifted, the ground took on a rosier hue. We were walking toward the amazing presence of Huascarán, the highest peak in Peru. The ravine opened up toward the base of the mountain and Marc Antonio pointed.

"See them?" he said. "A pair of foxes."

"Where? Where?"

He kept pointing. I thought I made out a gray blur but wasn't sure.

"Oh, come on," I laughed. "What color are their eyes?"

"They say the fox has a power," said Eusebio, "to take away human speech. He has the power in his tail. From the moment you spot him and he sees you, he makes you mute. He won't let you speak until he leaves. That's what they say."

"But I just spoke."

Eusebio's eyes crinkled up as he smiled. "You're lucky he didn't see you."

By the time we thought of lunch, the sun had burned off the cloud cover and my face was on fire. The sun on the snow the day before had given me a sunburn despite my hat. We made our way toward a grassy spot, and Eusebio pointed to the ground. A wonderful cactus-like pin cushion held a glorious gaudy red flower. On closer examination, the pin cushion was made up of a thousand tiny cactuses, all growing together.

"Huácuru Huayta," said Eusebio. "Cactus flower. Be careful not to sit on it no matter how soft it looks."

He very carefully plucked the flower and handed it to me. The traitorous needles at its base were made up for by the gorgeous redness. I tucked it into my hatband. It looked like it might have come from a South Sea island.

After lunch we pushed on at a smart pace. With every degree

of descent my body grew stronger and more agile. Alfonso's clop clop clop accompaniment picked up speed and I felt I could run until the end of the night, until my body dropped in its tracks. The sun beat down relentlessly, the air was dry. I tied a handkerchief across my nose to protect my face and ran, euphoric.

We caught up to an old man with a burro. It was our friend— the blue hat! He joined our band. Marc Antonio led the burros out in front. It was a day made for walking. The brilliant white shoulder of Huascarán stood in sharp contrast to the perfectly blue sky; an ácaca bird swooped in her weaving pattern from rock to rock.

When the ravine opened onto the Huaylas valley, we quit the trail and turned southward into the shadow of the glacier Hualcán. Hualcán, as nearly as I could make out, meant yoke or necklace. Its shallow roundness mirrored the wide white interwoven necklaces the women in the towns through the Huaylas valley wore—to represent their wealth, or marital status, or their joy in being beautifully adorned.

We came upon a vine growing up the papery bark of a quenhual tree and out to its branches. It looked like a passion flower vine, but the flowers were round and red. Marc Antonio picked one for me. He said the vine was called Pomegranate of Foxes. Like the cactus, Huácuru Huayta, it gave a little fruit that quenched the thirst of a walker.

"Why Pomegranate of Foxes? Can they climb up there?"

Marc Antonio laughed. "No, but foxes get thirsty too."

We made camp at the Auquismayo, which meant Old River. It came down from the headlands between Hualcán and another glacier, Chequiaraju. Its source, Juan said, was Old Lake at the top of Old Lake Ravine. That made sense. The old man went off to see if the river would give us fish for dinner.

I claimed the space behind a huge boulder as my bathroom. Hopping over the needle sharp grass, I stepped into the river. The turquoise water leaped and splashed over red gold rocks. A dragonfly positioned himself on a shelf in the afternoon light. All my strenuous effort ran off into the water.

The brush at the water's edge made a dark respite from the relentless sun. Upstream, a small waterfall churned the water and charged the air. All the angles in me relaxed. I washed, dressed, and sat on a rock in the swirling water. A fly walked into the sunlit spray. I thought how lucky we were to come leaping and jumping down from the heights to this gurgling stream. Vitality born of action accepted everything in its path—violence, tenderness, sun, shadow—and kept on going.

For my companions, Pachamama, the earth mother Goddess, was the one to thank for everything. The way they offered the first food to the fire, or the first sip of water to the earth, or threw a party for their fields, or saluted the presiding spirits in a new place. It sprang from a love and reverence I felt as well. From vastly different cultures we both sang to her; the words might be different, but the song was the same.

Over our dinner of fresh fish and boiled potatoes, the old man voiced his concern for a man from his village, who had gone up alone to the pass the day before. He had not met him coming down and hoped he had made it safely through the tunnel before the landslide. I thought of the blood I'd envisioned dotting the snow, and the feeling I'd had that someone had died, and said nothing.

As night fell, dozens of fireflies did a weaving dance around us in the dark and mixed with the sparks from the fire. The portable altar in my tent consisted of a candle affixed to a flat rock, surrounded by all the flowers I had gathered that day. I loved being in the enclosed space. The little acts of sewing, working on my notes, or arranging my gear for the next day took on a quiet, calm importance.

The old man had squeezed into the tent with my three companions; I could hear their laughter as he accommodated himself in the crowded space. I lit the bundle of sage and sweet grass and offered the smoke to the four directions, above and below. A wind started up, then the crackle of rain as it hit the tent. Where would I go if the fox stole my voice? I wanted only to offer my thanks to the places I was passing through. That was all I wanted to say.

In the morning the grass had lost its sharp edges to the softening rain. Our friend and his burro had left at dawn. Marc Antonio greeted me with his hand out; on his palm was a long thin feather.

"From the ácaca," he said. "She left it on a rock."

Down one half of the feather's length were yellow and gray stripes; the other half was all gray. The shaft stood out in brilliant yellow.

He handed me the feather. "It's for you."

I thought of putting it in my hatband. But at the end of each day my hat was crowded with all the flowers and leaves I'd gathered, and once I arranged them around an altar, I left them there. I started each morning fresh with an empty hat. To keep the feather, I needed a more permanent arrangement.

In the shamanic techniques I'd been learning, we'd used a rattle to salute the four directions, the sky, the earth, and ourselves. I remembered the *curandero* rattling over us through the night in the Amazon jungle. I thought of buying a gourd in the market when I returned to the valley, and tying to it everything I found that I wanted to keep. I would honor the powers of the place by tying their gifts together, and taking them with me when I left. The feather could be the beginning.

On the other side of the river, an ácaca bird was looping up the steep slope. "Ácaca, ácaca, brrrr," she cackled.

Faldeando, crossing the skirts of the mountains at a brisk pace, was every bit as strenuous as Eusebio predicted. Every hilltop outlined on the sky was followed by a downward push; then up again, and so on. Some of the slopes had been used by shepherds with their flocks. I came across strands of brightly colored yarn and stuffed them in my pocket for the rattle.

I had often seen the native women making thread on a spindle as they walked along, from the wool of sheep, llama, or alpaca. They usually carried a baby on their back and herded the flock as well. The thread they made was woven into blankets, or knitted into sweaters, socks, or hats to sell to tourists. For their own clothes they seemed to prefer the brightly dyed yarn they had to buy in the market. That was what I was finding on the ground.

To the east of us was the changing profile of the glacier Hualcán, the necklace; before us was one of the peaks of Copa. Traversing the high slopes gave a much bigger piece of sky than hiking through the *quebradas*. We watched one cloud move in like a white wing sweeping the far-off slope, which was tawny and dry. Eusebio said the rainy season was the only time all the hills were green.

Behind us was the white head of Huascarán, the highest mountain in Perú. He was also called El Maldito, the Wicked One, by the inhabitants of the Huaylas valley because of the avalanche and mudslide of 1971. An earthquake, whose epicenter was off the coast of Peru had shaken the mountains; one whole section of Huascarán's glacier had come crashing down into Llanganuco Lake.

What the people in the towns below saw was a huge wall of mud, rocks, and water coming at them at incredible speed. Few survived. The entire city of Yungay was buried, except for the tops of four palm trees in the town square. The whole area where the city had stood was *tierra santa,* holy ground, a cemetery, and no one was permitted to build there.

Angling into a fold in the hillside, we came to a stand of trees with glorious yellow flowers. Close examination showed long stamens amid petals that started pale yellow, blended with pink, and grew to bright peach at the edges. As showy and luxurious as peonies, they numbered about a hundred on each small tree.

"Salta Perico," said Eusebio, giving me one for my hat."You see, the tree gives flowers at the same time as seeds. It can't afford to waste any time."

Salta meant jump, and *perico,* as far as I knew, was a bird; I couldn't make any sense of it, unless the seeds exploded from the pods. The empty dry pods were also extraordinary. They were crook-necked, open bellied, and ended in a long swallow tail. Looking up into the flowers, I heard a clicking noise. Some empty seedpods were knocking against each other.

"I'm collecting things for a rattle," I said.

Eusebio's eyes twinkled. "For a baby or yourself?"

"What would a baby want with these things? It's for me."

"Then the dry ones give a better sound. The older ones."

He helped me pick a dozen. Hiking out, we saw Alfonso, Juan, and Marc Antonio a quarter mile ahead along the hillside. Eusebio pointed to a distant stand of eucalyptus trees where we would stop for lunch. The blue-green splotch was a welcome respite from the bright sere landscape. My calves and thighs from the week on the trail were singing as we marched along.

In the shade of the grove we had our lunch of canned tuna fish, onion, and bread. White cheese and one apple apiece. My companions had been drinking from any clear stream, but I carried my own canteen of water treated with chlorine and hydrogen peroxide. I preferred that taste to iodine-treated water, and it worked just as well against antamoeba coli, an intestinal parasite I frequently brought back from my travels. It did not, I was told, protect against giardia, which reputedly laid eggs in the liver.

"Alfonso has the life," said Marc Antonio. "He eats as he goes, and his pack gets lighter as our food runs out."

"Runs out?" Juan countered. "Didn't you taste it running past your tongue?"

The truth was we were low on supplies. The landslide had added two whole days to our journey. Eusebio got out the map. The three of them discussed distances and walking speeds. Once we got closer to the Honda valley, Juan and Marc Antonio would circle down to Vicos and buy supplies, while we hiked over the headlands and entered the gorge from above. We would meet at a place several hours up the canyon.

I was glad I was not going down. The cumulative effect of all the days out had made me more at one with the land, and more alert with my physical senses. The past was gone, the future did not exist. Like Alfonso, every day my baggage got a little lighter. In the space it left I was more alive. I did not want to give that up for a kilo or two of potatoes.

Marching all afternoon, we surprised one tiny deer on a headland dense with thickets. The *venado* was half the size of a white-tailed deer, but his eyes seemed much larger. He jumped over the lip of ground and bounded downhill. Though hunting was forbidden in the Cordillera Blanca National Park, the *venado* were not as plentiful as they once had been.

We were huffing up another slope.

"Wait, wait," I said, "let me guess. What could be on the other side of this hill? Don't tell me now. Could it be another downhill to a crevice, and then another hill?"

It seemed like we had climbed fifty slopes since the morning. My legs were feeling more like spent anchors than long lean walking machines.

"Ah, but what you don't know is, we're not going down." Eusebio pointed. "Out on that promontory, see it? Like little houses along the line of trees?"

"What is it?"

"Amápampa. Field of the Ancient Ones." He chuckled, "You could say it's where they are sleeping."

"We're camping out in a graveyard?"

"The graves have long since been emptied, but the *chulpas* remain."

Chulpa was the word in Quechua for the stone enclosures where mummies were interred in Incan and Pre-Incan times.

We reached the little plateau facing the Cordillera Negra as the pink gold sun was going down. Along the line of eucalyptus woods ran a small clear stream; in among the trees was a plentiful supply of dry wood. When I got back with my wash and an armful of branches, the tents had been set up and the fire was sending out showers of sparks in the darkness.

Juan was the head architect of the tents, Eusebio was our master chef, and Marc Antonio the chief water carrier and bottle washer. I was the wood gatherer and helped at cleaning up. We sat on four separate stones around the fire. The meal was starchy noodles with onions and garlic.

"Ooo-ooo." It sounded like an owl.

Marc Antonio looked over his shoulder. *"Tucu,"* he said.

Eusebio laughed. *"Tucu* or *cucu,* now, make up your mind."

Tucu, Eusebio said, was owl in Quechua, but *cucu* meant a spirit.

"I don't know," said the boy. "I'm not going over there to find out."

The mountains behind us held the glow of sunset long after we'd been sitting in darkness. Eusebio had a battery-powered flashlight like a miner's lantern that he strapped onto his head when he was cooking. He said it was standard gear for mountaineers. I thought he looked wildly funny, like a resident gynecologist for Outward Bound, but I had to admit it was practical.

The lantern was flickering.

"It's the wires," he said. "Not getting enough contact."

"I have a saw blade on my knife you could use to pare them down," I said.

"Can I penetrate your tent?"

His choice of words was not lost on me. I smiled broadly. "Of course you can."

The terrain made the day before look like a rain forest. The land was scorched and hard, the vegetation bleached and dusty. Sticks and leaves crackled like cellophane underfoot. One drop of water was so precious. The canteen on my back was my lone defense against the sure death promised by the land.

We'd settled into a pattern of the father and son out in front with Alfonso, and Eusebio and I behind. As I scrabbled up a slope, Eusebio whistled a sweet tune, like a serenade. It came, I thought, from his love of the land. The ease between us was innocently flirtatious. Penetrate my tent? Sure. But I was happy to feel free from any needs or desires.

We passed a stubbly bush with small white flowers. I picked one. It smelled like feet.

"She'kia," he said. "Good for dislocations."

Juan and Marc Antonio waited for us at the top of the ridge on a toppled stone wall. The crazy Inca, I thought, building temples in such inaccessible places! Across the way was a slope equally precipitous; from either, one could see fifty miles out over the valley. I realized the crumbling ruin had once been a watch tower, a strategic lookout post.

Four hawks circled overhead. There was a death component in the dry wind, the thorn bushes, and stony ground. My solar plexus relaxed into the certitude of my own death—perhaps not then and there, but certainly and inevitably somewhere. An ácaca bird cackled and whistled. I located her, preening on the wall. The ruins, overgrown with dusty trees and bushes, spread like railroad rooms along the ridgeline.

It was such an abandoned corner. *Condormarca,* Eusebio called it. Place of the condor. I could imagine turtles, snakes, and scorpions making their rounds, and the death rattle of each of them as the condor attacked. Or the fox ran laughing down the hill with their voice. The desert wind brought a tiny sound like somebody's voice. A real voice. We all looked up at once.

A dot silhouetted against the sky was waving to us from the steep hill opposite. Eusebio said it was a shepherd boy with his dog. His flocks must have been below the rock he stood on. Marc Antonio, whose eyes were keenest, said he had a slingshot in his hand. The wind carried what we had of a dialogue across the abyss. It sounded like Motu was his name. We shouted and waved for several minutes, then he jumped down to his flock and was lost to view.

We made our way down a steep incline toward a line of trees. Juan and Marc Antonio angled with the burro along the periphery. Eusebio and I went straight down the bowl. My nostrils widened at the presence of water. Just listening to the gurgling sound was refreshing. Crashing out of the underbrush, we came to a tunnel of trees. A turquoise river bounded over rocks in a narrow channel. I squatted on the bank. The energy was wild. It was one of those rivers that could take you down in a second and keep laughing all the way to the valley below.

"Come on," Eusebio urged. "Follow me over the rocks."

I wanted to stay right there. To fill my canteen and talk to the river, maybe bury a gift on the bank.

"Come on, Juan will be waiting. We have two hours yet to the campsite."

He looked very handsome in the shady tunnel. I followed his lead, rock to rock, securing myself on one before hopping to the next. The last leap was the widest. On the bank he held out his hand for me. As I landed, my sunglasses fell from my pocket. His outstretched hand swooped down and grabbed them, inches from the water. It was quite a catch. Grinning, he handed them over. I suddenly felt like kissing him. We stood there for a second. I adjusted my pack. The moment passed.

We followed the river down to where two deep channels had been cut to branch out from the river. By the simple maneuver of fitting a square rock into one channel, the water was diverted to irrigate other fields in the community below. Eusebio said it was usually someone's job to come up in the early afternoon, and move the boulders to change the course of the water. It was glacial melt in the White Range that provided water in the dry winter, thus giving the people two growing seasons.

We caught up with Juan and Marc Antonio on the path that led up to the Vicos glacier and the lake at its feet. A teenage boy came running down. On his hat and inside his open shirt he carried a quantity of Rima Rima, the gorgeous rosy flowers of the frosty heights. The boy had evidently just gathered them, by their freshness.

Eusebio asked if he could part with one for *La Señora*, meaning me. The boy laughed and said he had none to spare. By the way he clutched them to his chest and hurried past us, I knew he was headed for his girlfriend, or perhaps his mother, to whom he wanted to give the whole glorious bouquet.

We made our camp on a jutting headland overlooking the Callejón de Huaylas. Behind us was the gleaming shoulder of Huascarán; unseen below was Vicos, a sizeable village. When Sendero tried to infiltrate the mountain valleys and control the passes, the people of Vicos had caught two of them and beaten them to death with sticks. As Eusebio explained, the community already had the cooperative spirit the Shining Path was trying to foster, and did not want outsiders coming in and telling them what to do. Nor did they want the government, which had flocked to the area after the earthquake, to interfere. The community had acted as a single entity in asking for loans to clean up the thermal baths of Chancos, a tourist attraction, and to buy a truck for the iron ore from their mines inside the canyon.

Each family had its own small fields and private holdings; but the flocks, mines, and precious woodlands were held in common. Unlike most Peruvian *campesinos,* they had enough land and opportunities to offer a future to their young. They controlled the entire Honda valley all the way up to the pass and knew everything that happened in it.

"That's the best alternative I've heard," I said, "to the pure disdain of the government and to Sendero. Are there any more communities like Vicos?"

"They are the biggest," said Juan, "but there are others. E'qash, across from the town of Carhuaz; Huapra, to the north of Huaraz; Olleros to the south; and Huancapampa, by the town of Catac. All in the Callejón de Huaylas."

"So Sendero gets no foothold in them?"

Juan shrugged. "The last two that came through Vicos were not killed."

"Perhaps they wished they had been, though," said Eusebio, "when they arrived at the police station."

They both laughed.

I came out of the tent to a gloriously sunny morning. Dwarfed by the boulder next to which he had built the fire, Eusebio sat alone. Juan and Marc Antonio had apparently left, taking everything except my tent and the pot he was stirring.

"Looks like they got an early start," I said.

"That's for you." He pushed the pot of oatmeal toward me. "We've already eaten. You and I have a six hour walk before we meet them up the *quebrada.*"

"I bet you they get there first."

After an hour's trek we came to the lip of a bowl that dropped abruptly. It looked like impenetrable jungle to me, but Eusebio led the way down the vertical wall by the faintest of animal trails. I kept the likelihood of my tumbling over the edge to myself. At closer range I saw the whole hillside was crisscrossed by trails, though most were narrow and only waist high. Clawing through, I caught the acrid smell of dense vegetation I knew from the jungle.

At the bottom of the valley floor he picked a path through the stifling overgrowth. Unable to see my way out, I stayed close behind him. It wasn't exactly claustrophobia; more like fear of being swallowed alive.

Suddenly he stopped and pointed to the ground. "Look at this." There were small white bones in the dirt and what looked like a canine skull. "Fox," he said.

We scrabbled through the dust collecting the bones. Besides the skull there was a jawbone, scattered teeth, and several round hollow vertebrae. Under some leaves was a claw. The skull was small; the fox had been just a pup when it died.

"Looks like he ventured too far from the den, for someone so little."

Eusebio nodded. "Whoever ate him, did it right here."

I arranged the bones on the ground in what looked like their rightful order, but the tail was missing. He checked the underbrush slowly and carefully in all directions. After some minutes, he shook his head.

"No, no tail." He helped me pile them into my handkerchief. "You get everything but the voices."

Out of the bowl, we crossed the headlands south toward Quebrada Honda, Deep Ravine. To circumvent the steep walls of the gorge, we made our way down past walled and rocky pasture land until we reached a road. The dusty highway in the mountains' domain seemed so incongruous. It was built by the people of Vicos to go by truck to their mines.

Everywhere was the evidence of an industrious people: the rock walls, tended road, the eucalyptus seedlings planted where trees had been cut. Around a bend the valley widened to a long grassy pasture where llamas, goats, sheep, cows, and a few bulls were grazing. A shepherd in brightly colored clothes stood watching her flock from the edge of the field. Behind her, the newborn lambs and goats were jumping straight up from the rocks.

Eusebio pointed to the glacier up the valley. "That's Rataquenua."

"Does it flank the pass we would have crossed?"

He nodded. "On the other side is Paccharaju: Peak of the Waterfall. It takes its name from Yanapaccha, black waterfall, that pours down its flanks."

"That'll be our view at the top?"

"No. In front of Paccharaju is another glacier we'll see from our camp. Yaku Huarmi. It means Woman of Water."

I smiled broadly.

"I knew you would like that."

The sky clouded over and the air grew cool. The flat wide road was such a change. I could look at the landscape instead of my feet. We heard the truck behind us laboring up the hill a full quarter hour before it appeared. The ancient thing was bound for the mines, empty except for three helpers who waved from the back. We were really covering ground. A man came toward us leading two donkeys. He'd just come over the pass from Callejón de Canchucos. He'd passed our friends an hour ahead of us up the road. He said villagers in the Ulta valley had found a man buried in the landslide. I sent up a prayer for the man who had shared our trail.

The precipitous slopes closed in; Deep Gorge was aptly named. The rollicking river was the Hondamayo, Deep River. Eusebio pointed to the narrowest waist of valley ahead. It was La Portada, the porch, or doorway: another entrance to the mountains' empire. Behind us the land held a V of sky.

At La Portada, a ten foot high hurricane fence stretched from the slope to the river's edge. GATE CLOSED AFTER DARK, read the sign. A man with a rifle came from the cottage behind the gate. With the steep slopes and the roaring river, I could see how the Vicos people kept control of all movement through the valley. The man nodded and waved us through.

The families of Vicos took turns manning the gate, Eusebio said. They spent three months at a stretch away from their village, pasturing flocks and keeping an eye on traffic from the east. Across the field one tent was set up. Marc Antonio was waving with his hat. They had a fire pit already dug at the base of the boulder.

"Welcome to Punco Pampa," said Marc Antonio. It meant Field by the Door.

I took the towel from my pack and hurried to wash before dark. The river was red and roared over boulders; I was looking for something more protected. In a bowl of rocks I found a tiny bay. The slightest ruffling of water touched the grasses and round rocks at the edge with a fine red dust.

I jumped down. Over the boulder at my back, the water surged past wildly—tons of water directly overhead—without entering my chamber. I stepped gingerly into the pool at my feet. Another perfect bathtub.

The night was alive with fireflies. We had boiled potatoes, beets, and cheese omelets. I asked if they'd brought back any *granadilla*, passion fruit. It had been in all the markets when we'd left.

"Aumi, Maymay," said Eusebio.

"What?"

Marc Antonio grinned. "It means, Yes, Mother."

"Aumi, Maymay?"

Eusebio nodded. "And you know how you answer?"

"Aumi, Taytay," said Marc Antonio.

"Aumi Taytay?"

The boy went into peals of laughter. "Yes, father. That's what it means. *Aumi Taytay.*"

I looked at the three of them sitting on our half circle of stones by the fire.

"And you're not going to tell me how to say no?"

Juan piled more wood on. The flames shot up as high as the boulder. Inside my tent I could see without using a candle. On a flat rock I put the fox's bones, the ácaca feather, and the salta perico seed pods tied with yarn. My altar was getting crowded.

Was it the spirit of the earth I was worshipping? Was it the fox? It was and it wasn't. Threading the mountains over Pachamama had taught me in ways I couldn't define. Everything that informed my being and opened me up made me grateful. The pungent smoke from my sage and sweet grass mixed with the smoke from the fire.

Coming out to the blue light of dawn, I saw Marc Antonio by the kitchen boulder. He pressed his finger to his lips and pointed. Two gray foxes were running together across the field. Their ears were standing up, half again the size of their head. Their coats blended in with the mist on the ground. They disappeared behind the taulli bushes, came out by the road, and headed up the valley.

I looked at Marc Antonio. "We're lucky," he said. "The wind was in our favor. This place should be called Atuk' Pampa."

"Atuk' is fox? Field of the foxes?"

He grinned. "You are learning."

We were packed and on the road by eight. Climbing past fields enclosed by stone walls, we could see the *andenes* across the way—

the terraces carved into the precipitous slopes to make use of every inch of arable earth. Cows grazed unattended at the river's edge.

An hour up the valley we reached Yana Paq'sa, the famous waterfall that came down between two mountains. On the left was Paccharuri, High Field of the Waterfall; on the right, Paccharaju, Glacier of the Waterfall. Both took their names from the cascade plummeting down the slope and across the huge boulder, cutting white channels into its face like curly hair.

By late afternoon we had reached the narrow bowl at the top of the valley. Called Rinconada, Corner, it was hemmed in on three sides by walls that climbed straight up to the rim. On the road we passed a newly built rustic chapel, open in the front like a Catskill lean-to. Inside was a six foot cross made of leaves, stalks, and dried flowers. Eusebio said he'd heard of a priest who'd been working with people throughout the valley; perhaps he was responsible for the chapel.

We made camp beyond the stream, by a boulder in the field of taulli and grazing cows. At twilight a man came towards us from the house we'd seen by the road. His daughter, trailing shyly behind him, wore a full red skirt, a red jacket, and a red and black carrying blanket on her shoulders. She looked about six. On her hat was a grand bouquet of Rima Rima.

They lived there year round, the man said. His wife had just had a baby and was unable to meet us. He pointed to a yellow machine that looked like a back hoe, parked under a ledge beyond his house. It had been brought in, he said, by the priest to grade a new road up to the pass. Eusebio pointed out the pass up to the left, Portachuelo de Honda, that we knew from the Ulta side.

But Sendero had threatened the priest's life, the man said, and blown up another machine right in front of him. The priest had been committed to the road and to bringing hydro-electric energy to the region, but he'd had to retreat to the valley until times were safer. Our friend was the nominal caretaker of the back hoe, idle for more than a year.

I wondered aloud if the landslide we'd met on the Ulta side had been other than a natural occurrence.

Eusebio translated into Quechua.

The man shrugged in reply.

That night after dinner I stayed up late, arranging my altar with the candles, flowers, bones, and seeds. When my companions went to sleep and the fire died, I came out to the stars appearing one by one over the fireflies. I found a constellation I didn't know and checked it with my flashlight on the star map. Lupus, the Wolf. I clicked off the light. On the lip of the precipice up to the pass Yaku Huarmi, The Woman of Water, was shining against the sky.

Climbing up from camp in the early morning, we passed a thin waterfall tumbling over the brink above us. When we gained the rim of the bowl, we could see below us the three C's of civilization: *carpa, casa,* and *capilla.* The tent, the house, and the little chapel. The wet wall flanking the path was covered with plants and tiny flowers.

Above Rinconada was another wider bowl. The road to the pass angled up to the left, but the wall we approached was the most spectacular. A gigantic spout of water gushed from a hole in the center of the rock face. Tons of water per second shot out in an arc forty horizontal feet before crashing down to the river below. As we neared it the roar got louder, the energy of the water more impressive. It was this stupendous force the priest had wanted to harness for electric power. From above, the spout was hidden by an ordinary jumble of boulders. All that was left of its voice was muffled thunder.

Before us the last long valley climbed to where the glaciers stood, shoulder to shoulder. The puna grass was a tawny color, interrupted by boulders and wandering streams. Eusebio pointed out how the cattle were grouped along the edges of the field; through the center ran a bog impossible to cross. He had gotten stuck once returning from the glacier Yanarangra, and had had to bivuoac against a hill until morning.

We skirted the northern edge of the valley along a narrow track that climbed steeply above the fields. A racket up the hill caught our attention. Two baby hawks were flapping in the air, guided by their mother who was squawking from a rock. From the commotion of their wings, translucent in the sunlight, it must have been their virgin flight. At last one fledgling gained the air, then the other, while the mother followed with her eyes.

The trail gained altitude winding in and out along the skirt of the mountain. Tramping around a bend, we startled a bull at his lunch, who crashed down the slope away from us at a fearsome speed. Juan said the cows who pastured that high got used to the terrain, but less and less used to people. After a few years, they could not come down to corrals again. They would have grown too wild.

The hillsides and slopes became crowded with lupine. I buried my face in the flowers. The deep musky scent made me think of a woman who growled when she made love, though you would never think it, gazing into her cornflower blue eyes.

Eusebio pointed to two glaciers across the way: Chinchay and Yanarangra. He showed us the lines of ascent and the campsites. His face came alive. The third, Palcaraju, he had scaled with a French expedition. We would see it if we climbed a bit higher.

"Why do you need to go up?" I asked.

"To the top?" He turned his gaze back to the glaciers. "To be closer to God," he said quietly. "To look and look and look until you lose yourself in that joy." I understood exactly.

I did not join them to see the third glacier. For me the taulli was enough. This was the bowl beyond the pass: there was nothing to scale, no goal to reach. I was happy to sit in the scent of blue flowers and watch the cows below. The white mountain gulls that accompanied the herd were screeching so loud, like women in the market passing the news by Radio Bemba. I was happy to sit and eat my lunch and think about nothing.

When my friends returned, we started our march down the valley. We passed the mines. By late afternoon we stood again over Rinconada, where the chapel, tent, and house made a triangle far below. The men stayed to gather herbs from the rock face. Marc Antonio and I led Alfonso down.

It was no accident that the ácaca came to where I squatted in the morning, behind the taulli bush. It was no accident that she screeched and cackled above me as I washed in the river. The sun spread wide and sweet over Yaku Huarmi: it was time to go. The lightning bugs were loathe to leave the tent; I was slow in packing my things. There was no way around it, we were going down.

"What about the condors?" I asked, as we tramped toward La Portada. I pointed to four birds circling high above us.

My companions stopped. Two more condors came. Far off another circled, and soon we counted eight condors, homing in on something. Eusebio said a cow had gotten caught too high on the ledges and had fallen. Now it was either dead or dying. They located the body by the circling birds.

We sat to watch. Eusebio showed how the male had a white neck, and white on his wings, which distinguished him from the female. Now there were ten condors sitting in nearby trees, or circling down. They must've had their own Radio Bemba.

Back on the road we overtook a man and boy leading a yoked ox. The boy looked to be about ten. They were the family caretaking La Portada. The father was going from plot to plot of his own land, plowing it in readiness for the seeds. Soon the rains would come. The boy pointed to a puddle of water just off the road.

"Mineral water," he said. "See the bubbles?"

We bent over the water hole. A tiny fountain of sparkling water was shooting up from the earth. Juan took out the canteen and filled it up. Since it came straight from the earth, I filled my canteen as well. The water, tasting faintly of sulphur, had a splendid effervescence.

The men and Marc Antonio strode ahead with the burro and ox, while I lagged behind. I wasn't tired. I simply did not want to leave. The little boy kept me company. I asked him as we walked along how long he would stay away from the village. Was he missing school?

"I'm taking an artistic vacation," he said. "While I'm here I look around, I watch what's going on." He pointed above us. "I know that mountain, and that one. I've been to the lake up by Paccharuri. I've been to the lake below Pucaranra. I've seen a lot."

I told him about the condors eating the cow.

"They probably pushed her off the ledge," he said, "because they were hungry."

"Can they do that?"

"They are very big, you know. They did it to me once when I was little, about three years old. I was playing at the edge of a drop, like this." He motioned to an eight foot bank to our left. "The condor came, he flew at me, right at me. All I could see were his wings flapping, and I fell off the edge."

"Were you scared?"

"Of course I was! They are very big, you know."

"And what happened?"

"I started screaming and my father came. He was waving a blanket and the condor flew up. I was lucky. Little animals and kids can disappear."

I began to laugh. "Aww, think of the poor guy just getting ready for a tender little bite."

His eyes sparkled. "Like a little pig or a baby lamb. The poor condor."

We left the father and son at La Portada and kept going until we reached the wide wooden bridge over the river. In the shade of two Salta Perico trees, Eusebio prepared lunch. I went off to be by myself.

Walking along the river, I thought of all the years I'd been coming to the Andes. After nearly two weeks I felt like I belonged again. I looked across the wild river at the sunny slope and felt like crying. You have been the arena of my life, I thought, lesson by lesson, year after year. What can I give in the face of your generosity? Nothing small will do. Can I give my heart to a land mass, to a river? Does that make me sentimental?

I picked up a round yellow rock, still warm from the sun on the riverbank, and laughed out loud. No matter what I said, or what I meant, the land like a mother was still giving to me, and I was still taking. I pocketed the stone.

At the boulder Marc Antonio handed me a delicate three petaled carmine flower. It could've been a cousin to the trilium. He said it was called Huac'anka, the flower that cries. Perhaps the drop of dew that rolled from the slender throat to the petal's edge looked like a tear.

I put it in my hat. He and Juan went to the river to wash our gear. I picked two Salta Perico blossoms, and tucked them next to Huac'anka in my hatband. Eusebio returned with something in his hand.

The gorgeous red and yellow cactus, Huácuru Huayta, with the traitorous needles at its stem. Eusebio did a curious thing. He asked for my hat, and stuck the flower into the band himself. In the center of the flower, which usually closed as soon as it was picked, he inserted a tiny twig to keep it open. My hat had a complete bouquet.

We marched down the valley to the pasture land, and the assorted herds grazing at eleven thousand feet. Just as we passed the shortcut to the village, the ácaca called behind us. She flew cackling from one side of the canyon to the other. Then she swooped back up the valley, with her yellow feathers flashing beneath her wings.

We were walking four abreast down the road at a rapid pace, reminding my toes they were definitely pressing against leather. When I ran down a steep incline, the Huácuru Huayta in my hat brim began to buzz. The little twig in the center vibrated in the wind like a bumblebee. Eusebio was grinning. We hurried past planted fields, stone walls, and carefully tended water channels that irrigated the hillside. Alfonso was clopping behind us as we reached the first house.

"Listen," said Eusebio. His head was cocked toward the direction of the sound with a questioning look in his eyes. Had I heard it? Behind the stone and adobe walls, from deep within the house it came.

Yes, I'd heard it. The first radio.

The Old Way

On a visit to Prague during the Velvet Revolution, I discovered in the National Museum on Wenceslas Square a whole room full of Mother-worship statues dating from 5000 B.C. to 330 B.C. from all over Eastern and Western Europe and the Middle East. The devotion invested in the tiny figures over such a wide span of time seemed so simple and universal. Wasn't anything written from then until now that celebrated or at least acknowledged her presence? Back in the United States, a friend suggested I read about Hinduism.

I learned that Shiva and Shakti were the male and female sides of God, and that everything in the universe was born of that union. The book went on to catalog male attributes for three hundred pages and female attributes for thirty-five pages, but the multiplicity was daunting. Much as I loved reading about Párvati, the goddess of mountains, and Annapurna, the goddess of food, they seemed like brilliant splinters. What I wanted was the whole radiant pie.

Male priests in churches and temples had represented the official religions for at least the last five thousand years. Their patriarchal edicts overshadowed the Mother's dominion. I was looking for the heart of worship, not the brain. Where were the household altars tended by women that kept devotion alive among the people? A friend who had lived in Kathmandu suggested Nepal. I had never been East or seen the Himalayas with my own eyes and asked him how I should prepare for the trip. His answer was succinct.

"Take one or two things you love with you. Don't worry about it. You're going home."

On the plane from Amsterdam I met three other women traveling alone: Aneek, a Dutch mountain climber who had just scaled a 23,000 foot Himalayan peak with a team of women climbers; Dominique, a young Belgian woman; and Lyla, a make-up artist who lived in Amsterdam and New York. Through the twenty-six hour flight, which seemed to stop everywhere in the Middle East, we became acquainted. In Kathmandu we went together to the Thamel, a crowded neighborhood of market stalls, and took rooms in the same hotel.

It was August and still monsoon season. Every day the sky opened and drenched the city. Shortly after the downpour, the steamy deserted alleys of the labyrinthine bazaar (pronounced buzzer) would fill up again. Adults, children, children carrying children, bicycles, rickshaws, Brahma bulls, tractors, autos, porters bearing enormous loads, skinny wandering calves and dogs, motorcycles, trucks—within minutes a living sea flooded the streets. The accompanying din engulfed the senses. I was amazed there were so few accidents.

Every day I threaded my way through the Thamel toward Dubwar Square, the main downtown plaza, by a different route. Everywhere were shrines and little temples: on the corners, hidden in courtyards, built into the walls. I knew the three religions in Nepal were Hinduism, Bon Shamanism, and Buddhism.

What impressed me was the sweet veneration of the people. Every day they brought offerings to goddesses, buddhas, saints, and gods. Some statues were bathed in clarified butter, some dusted with saffron. Others stood amid a scattering of fresh geranium petals, marigolds, turmeric, cardamon, and rice. The practice seemed so tender and familiar.

When they passed an important or much loved deity, the people would touch it, or bow before it, then touch their own foreheads. One popular ikon in the market was a round orange lump, about knee-high, so coated with loving offerings it was unrecognizable. I couldn't even guess what lay underneath. Another was a gaping hole in a stone set into a wall; it looked like a grinning mouth, or a vagina with spikey teeth.

The greeting was *Namaste*. Holding your hands together, as though in prayer, you touched the index fingers to your forehead, a little above the space between the eyes, and saluted the spirit that dwelt inside whomever you addressed. Without knowing one word of Nepalese, I found *Namaste* to be my bridge and passport. Slowly I learned the numbers from some kids in the neighborhood, and some questions: How much? Where is? How far? The answers, however, escaped me.

After days of combing the alleys I was struck one afternoon by a detail. In the architecture scaled to human size, the oldest structures in the marketplace looked more like ornate temples than stores or houses. The door frames and windows were intricately carved with swirls and curlicues, animals, goddesses, and gods.

A vendor sitting crosslegged in a dark wooden stall amidst her wares or a face suddenly visible in the window of a building stood out like a jewel in its setting. Here the home or the store was a temple, and the spirit dwelling within each inhabitant was God. What a beautiful concept: adorning one's house not as a possessive act, but as an offering to the spirit within.

I ducked past a woman selling T-shirts, and entered the sudden quiet of an inner courtyard formed by five buildings. The washlines above held gaily colored saris. In the center was a small, elaborately carved stone temple. As I came in, an old man in a white dhoti was talking excitedly and waving his arms at the statue on the facing side. He didn't seem mad or dangerous. He beckoned for me to come nearer. When I did, he pointed to the statue, a dancing figure I thought might be Shiva. The dancer had a sensual feminine grace and powerful female thighs, but no breasts.

Despite his matted gray hair and bony chest, the old man's quick gestures were those of a much younger person. He threw a small handful of rice grains over the statue's head, and spoke rapidly. He touched the red powder at the dancer's feet, then touched his own forehead, leaving a red mark slightly above the space between his eyes. He looked at me.

I took the rice he proffered and bowed to the dancing figure. Mirroring the old man exactly, I threw the rice and brought the powder from the dancer's feet to my forehead. He nodded approval, and took me by the hand to the following statue. It was a seated male figure. The old man waved gaily as if to a neighbor across the courtyard. He selected a marigold from the tiny bouquet someone had left in the grating, and put it behind his own ear. I did the same. Smiling, he patted my shoulder and pushed me toward the next statue. A female figure with four arms was standing on what might've been a shell or a flower. One of her top hands held a flower, one of her bottom hands was open. I studied her for a long while, and wondered who she was.

When I looked up, the old man was gone. I was touched that he'd shared his offerings with me, a perfect stranger, and showed me how to worship in his way. I bowed to the goddess before me and left the marigold at her feet.

I headed out with Dominique for the Buddhist temple Bodinath, following the vague directions of our hotel owners. Walking through Kathmandu was a process of letting go. One arrived at the most frequented places—the stores, bazaars, and temples—by allowing oneself to be swept along by the people going that way. As we started down a long hill, I asked a woman if we were headed toward the temple. Yes we were, but it wasn't Bodinath. The crowds had steered us to Pasupatinath—a temple to Shiva.

The maze of alleys held a bustling market. Vendors in busy kiosks sold prayer beads, powders, ointments, twisted ribbons, glass bangles, incense, mirrors: offerings and adornments for the pilgrim. Gaudy statues looked down from places of honor in the crowded stalls. On the blistering sidewalk, a young mother laid her baby on a ratty piece of cloth. She rubbed him down with what looked like mustard oil while he howled in the sun. A cow passed nonchalantly, perilously close to the baby's head. No one shooed it away.

We reached a great wall with an open gate. The sign in the entry, ONLY HINDUS ALLOWED INSIDE, was five feet high. The gatekeeper resting his rifle on the ground looked serious. A man in a business suit had to leave his shoes with a porter and go in barefoot. No leather was allowed inside. A group from India left cameras with a vendor. No pictures either. Dominique and I stepped up to try our luck.

Inside the temple, just beyond the gatekeeper, was a huge calf covered with gold. Someone had said that Nandi, the sacred bull, was the devoted servant of Shiva, whom I assumed he was facing. But the hair on my arms stood up as I gazed at the bull's hindquarters, ten feet high, pointed towards us.

When I had divorced myself from the Judeo-Christian ethic, because it left too great a portion of myself as a woman unanswered, all the forbidden elements in the Bible took on a new interest. The owl woman, the queen of darkness, the undulating serpent, the monster in the sea—I could have been any of them. Now in front of us was the golden calf excoriated by the Levites in their land grab from the native people; it epitomized the distance one could go from God the Father, and Jahweh, the tribal despot.

I smiled at the gatekeeper. "Will you let us in? We're pilgrims."

The man pointed to his ear, and shook his head. He didn't understand English. He pointed to the sign again, then at us, and shook his head more emphatically.

Dominique suggested we try another door. Pasupatinath covered a lot of ground. Walking the wall, we came to several doors, but someone at each one denied us entry. We could hear people inside singing a song to Ram. A man of indeterminate age came toward us holding up his hand as though warding off a blow.

"Please," he said, "I ask no payment. If you are satisfied with me as your guide, you can contribute to my household. Let me explain to you the temple."

He was either drunk or a bit unsteady on his feet; but he spoke English and seemed intelligent. We accepted. He led us over a small stone bridge across the river Basmati, which he said flowed into the Ganges, and up the stairs to a row of six foot high stone temples. In the center of each was a phallic stone, set inside a circle—the lingam and yoni, he said. The male and female principles on which all the gods and goddesses were based. The temples seemed to march across the hill, one inside the other, like a hallway of mirrors.

Up the grassy embankment we climbed to a group of small huts. Inside the darkened interiors were bearded ascetics, surrounded by groups of men smoking what smelled like hashish in little pipes. One sadu, called the yogurt *baba,* who'd eaten nothing but yogurt since birth, had the most followers. They treated him with great reverence. He had about ten pounds of hair on his head, and a piercingly direct regard.

"If it's true," I said, "about the yogurt, he's probably eaten better than a lot of people we've seen today. I guess there are no holy women."

Dominique gave a wonderfully Gallic shrug. "Among the *babas, alors,* no women permitted."

The guide suggested we take the bench in the sun that looked over the wall directly into the temple. The people we'd heard singing were inside a pavilion. Ram, pictured with cobras rising over his head, was another name for Shiva, said the guide. I thought of the Goddess of Knossos, staring ahead with great cat's eyes as she held two snakes up, one in each hand. The guide said it was a holiday, the Festival of Cobras.

A troop of large monkeys clattered over a corrugated roof by the temple walls. There must have been thirty of them following the dominant male, who reached the middle of the bridge where a humble old man swept the ground with a flimsy broom. Standing his ground until the last of his pack, a nursing mother with her baby on her back, caught up, the monkey was aggressive to all passersby, and no one interfered with him. Clearly the temple was his terrain too.

The guide pointed to two houses built into the temple walls, where the terminally ill, attended by their families, came to die. Straddling the bridge we'd crossed were the burning ghats—little platforms over the river—where the bodies were cremated. Wood was piled systematically for maximum heat; the body placed on top was covered with straw to hold the heat in. It took four hours for the skull to explode and the body to be turned into ashes. Then it was dropped into the river. Downstream, people stood bathing and drinking the water in ritual purification.

Pasupatinath was one of the three great temples to Shiva a Hindu had to visit before he died. The physical immensity of building after building, gold covered rooftops, wall inside wall— the temple and the busy commerce it supported resembled a small city. Both a marketplace and spiritual center. To feel the weight and gravity of it in the lives of the people, from birth to death to birth again, I understood a term I'd heard once: mother temple.

Here was the trident stuck in the ground by the burning ghat, the golden cupolas, and the barefoot fire tender in cast-off clothes; the tight balls of the screaming monkey and the swollen glands of the female in estrus, glowing red. The red-eyed people waited by the wall with a crumpled female body, next in line for the fire. Babies held by their mothers in the river current slapped the water happily. The guide said four hundred rupees for the burning of the poor, one thousand for the rich, including music.

People streamed up and down the stairs from the river to the temple and back again. The song for Ram was gaining momentum—call and response, call and response—until I couldn't take in one more thing. Not one more detail. I looked at Dominique. Her face had turned bright red in the sun. Her eyes looked trapped.

"I can't stay any more," I said. "I have to go."

She nodded in reply. Down past the ghat and a glimpse of the grayish skull in the straw, the guide led us to a cobblestone plaza in the sun. A stone temple, twelve feet high, stood with four carved pillars and three sides open to the air. On the fourth side was a goddess with ten arms brandishing weapons. She had a wildly beautiful expression on her face.

"This is our goddess, Durga. She takes our sacrifices."

Inside was a three foot high lingam set within the stone yoni. The whole temple interior was a faded brown as of dried blood wearing away. A liquid of indeterminate color sat in a groove on the floor. He smiled proudly at the wonderfully carved building.

"Only male animals are sacrificed." He ticked them off his fingers: "Ducks, goats, sheep, roosters, water buffalo, bulls—one thousand and eight bulls."

A boy about four had hopped up into the temple. It was just his size. He was playing, totally absorbed with the lingam, caressing it in the blood-spattered chamber. Dominique shuddered. We paid the guide hurriedly and dashed around the nearest corner.

A small juice stand was shaded by trees. I squatted by the outside wall while Dominique ran in. The air seemed ten degrees cooler. A produce market had been set up in the green shelter of four tall trees. Women surrounded by fruits and vegetables sat on the ground in the small courtyard outside the temple walls. I breathed in relief. The woman nearest me stood up from her oranges on the cobblestones, and stretched luxuriously. Her sweater hitched up in front, revealing a belly button Solomon would have extolled in song. Glass bracelets tinkled on her coffee colored arms. Her long black hair wore a bright red flower.

In this ancient religion the male and female elements that worked to keep the universe in existence could also play. Pleasure was a sacred act and a holy office. As I understood it, the temple women of the Old Way had not been prostitutes, but priestesses of power and understanding. I could picture the woman before me as one of these.

Visibly calmer, Dominique emerged from the fruit stand. We

headed toward the rickshaw station just in time to see the last one pulling away. Sweating in the sun, we were instantly surrounded by a crowd of beggars—the maimed, the blind, the deformed—children and adults crowding in, holding their hands out, whining for money. When we scattered what change we had, the crowd got larger and pushed in closer, pulling at our clothes.

A rickshaw turned the corner. We jumped in without bargaining. In the shade of the interior I realized my hands were shaking. The wheel of life and death as portrayed in the temple, and the fatalistic acceptance of the people unnerved me. I was glad to leave it behind. Sinking back in my seat I caught the profile of the driver in the rear-view mirror. He bore an uncanny likeness to José, a lover I'd lived with for two years in Peru.

It was José's profile I'd watched on the train all night riding through Colombia while I read the Kabbalah. José's face in the bathroom in the train station, when I had screamed for a knife. The tiny red figure had come out in waves of pain, and I had cut the umbilical cord. I left the four inch fetus in the overflowing toilet. It taught me all I needed to know of the physical universe, tooth and claw. After the hospital, I would glance at him as I read in the dim light about the Tree of Life, and the deaths of oneself along every path. My understanding and acceptance became intertwined with his sleeping profile bobbing in the motion of the train.

Now here was his profile in the rickshaw, a direct reminder of my own inclusion on the wheel I was rejecting. Shiva was speaking in the mirror. Everything around and in us was the dance.

We got out at a restaurant. Seated at a table, I found myself unable to speak. Dominique looked concerned.

"Are you all right?"

No, I wasn't. I got up and moved toward the back in search of a bathroom. At a sink in the alcove I burst into tears. Leaning my head against the wall, I felt like I had an anvil on my heart, and cried openly, I couldn't say why. I dipped my hands into the water and wet my head. Perhaps I wanted the wheel to wear a kinder face.

"Women should wear long skirts, mid-calf at least. It is important they not expose their legs. Pants are not acceptable." That was the word in our hiker's manual. My friend Lyla, who had the other room on the roof of our small hotel, was eager to get started. She had checked into all the trails for their respective rainfalls during monsoon season, and came up with the Annapurna trek as the driest, with perhaps the fewest leeches.

Rainy season would not be over for a month. I was in no rush, but Lyla had much less time than I. She proposed we walk for one week. In the local coffee shop an Australian climber said even four days up the trail would get us to where we'd see Ngadi Chuli, Phungu, or Manaslu, if the sky cleared.

The names rolled off his tongue with a tenderness I recognized. Mountain walkers have it—the tone of voice reserved for a remembered friend, a lover, or respected adversary. After weeks or months of walking around or over a mountain, you get to know it in the Biblical sense. For me, Manaslu was like the name on a mailbox in the lobby of an apartment house: I couldn't know who it was until I went up.

We got trekking permits from the government office and relief maps of the Annapurna Himal. *Himal* means snow peak or range. Lyla, a world traveler, had never done any hiking, but she made up in enthusiasm what she lacked in experience. On the hotel roof at sundown we watched the armies of the night fly out—the fruit bats, as large as foxes, that hung all day from the mango tree down the street—while we debated every item in our packs.

The following afternoon we got off the bus in the heat of Dumre, the starting point for the Annapurna circuit, and found a porter who knew the way. He had us buy a generous supply of plastic to keep ourselves dry, and a basket to hold our heaviest items, which he would carry with a strap slung across his forehead. His name, as nearly as we could make out, was Mylar. He spoke almost no English.

We set out the next morning in our dowdy cotton skirts and hiking boots. The weather was like a sauna. We were heading up the Marsyangdi river valley that snaked northward, nine thousand feet to the plain of Manang. We would go as far as we could in four days, and return in three.

We forded the rushing streams, swollen with water, that poured into the Marsyangdi. We skirted the three foot deep muddy ruts in the road they said was passable in dry season. The valley spreading out on both sides of the Marsyangdi was bright green with new rice growing in terraced paddies. The watery soil at the edges of the terraces was held in by bush beans. Dragonflies circled lazily. Thousands of butterflies with quivering wings congregated in the mud.

Acceptable behavior, said the manual, was to keep our bodies covered from the neck to well below the knees whenever among people. At our first overnight stop in Paundi Davan, we walked along the river away from town to wash off the sweat of the day's trek. But at every secluded spot we found, people kept popping up—especially children, who stared and giggled. We finally walked out fully clothed into the river and washed ourselves under the water. Lyla changed into a black tent-like dress, and took any subsequent attention with sharp ill humor.

The drink in the roadside inns was sweet tea with boiled milk, called *chai;* but chafing under the loss of amenities, we chose, when it was available, bottled water. Carried up on the backs of porters, the water cost more the farther we walked. Our exasperation changed nothing, except to increase private discomfort. Lyla and I took turns striding out ahead, leaving the other behind with Mylar and the basket.

The *Namastes* increased. Merchants, pilgrims, porters, businessmen, students, grandmothers, children—everyone we passed on the road held their hands up to their forehead, looked us in the eyes and bowed to the spirit inside us, as we did them. After days, the effect was cumulative. In the brief sun dazzling on the water, in the old woman napping under her thatched roof, in the thousand shades of gray through the rainy afternoon, God was saluted everywhere, inside and outside the heart.

The hot humid weather changed to cool rain, and we still had not seen one mountain. People in the villages where we stopped would nod and point to a bank of clouds, indicating where the highest mountain stood, and call it by name. Lyla and I would look and believe them, of course, but see nothing. In Besisahar, she chose to wait out the last two days in a nice hotel with a shower and Western food, while I kept going with Mylar.

We left town in a heavy downpour and crossed the bridge to the east side of Marsyangdi Khola. *Khola* means river. Mylar said it was deeper than a man, and could carry a person off in its current. Below us the wild and frothy water looked like it could drag away trees and houses as well. I realized the landscape could never be taken for granted; awe and respect were natural conditions of survival.

By the time we reached Bhulebhule, a corridor of balconies hugging the river, my clothes and boots were soaking wet. We entered the inn of a fabulously beautiful Tibetan woman, whose small son followed her everywhere she went. The walls of the common room were lined with divans covered with blankets. The windows in the back wall overlooked the river; the doors to the street stood ajar until dark.

As night came on, the kerosene lamp on the table cast shadows on the lined face of the old man who sat next to me. Supper was the usual *daal baat,* rice and peas served on enormous aluminum trays. Everyone ate with their fingers. The customers besides myself were merchants and their porters, traveling to and from Manang. I guessed the porters slept on the divans, and the guests in the private rooms upstairs.

The second story was one large room divided into cubicles. Since I was the only woman and foreigner, I was surprised to find my own room had no door. I pulled the top mattress off the bed and leaned it upright to cover my doorway. Without the language I was at the mercy of circumstances. My understanding was limited, and my participation reduced to silent observation.

There had been no mountains and no views; more than likely

there would be none. My feet hurt. My boots would never dry by morning. I opened the windows to the sound of the river and the steady patter of rain from the eaves. I wondered if I should go on the next morning, or just turn back. I felt cut adrift from my purpose. Was I finding remnants of an old religion by walking in the rain?

I awoke at two in the morning to the sound of wind. Moonlight was pouring through the window. Northward, over the river, was a single glorious snow-capped mountain with a ring of clouds at its feet. I thought of the goddess Párvati, Daughter of the Mountain, standing completely revealed in the blue-white light. The moon was one day from the full.

I consulted the map. It was Manaslu. Like an answer to my questions, I decided on the spot that back in Kathmandu I would look for a guide who spoke English, one who could help me communicate with the people. I would return then to do the whole trek, if I could. I bowed to the mountain in its pillow of clouds. *Namaste, Manaslu. Namaste.*

Starting out at dawn, Mylar and I covered quite a bit of ground by noon. From the villages and isolated houses, more and more Buddhist prayer flags fluttered in the wind, and the faces looked more Tibetan. The morning fog lifted a little. Wisps of mist drifted up from the river. In the sober light, the hills and fields on both sides were a bright lush green. When the skies closed in again, it didn't matter. The glimpse of Manaslu gave resoluteness to my steps. I felt in harmony with the landscape, and myself as part of it. There was no better life than a walker's. No responsibilities except to the moment—to reach the ridge line, or make it to a bed by nightfall. I had only to stay open and take what came.

The house we stopped at for lunch belonged to a man who had once served in the British army. He suggested chicken as the best dish of the house. To my surprise he killed a chicken on the spot; with a knife like a scimitar he cut the raw flesh into slices. His home was new—evidently built on the trail for the trekking business—and paid for, I discovered later, by the prices he charged.

Up a walled ditch cluttered with garbage and excrement we made our way in the late afternoon. It was a steep climb up Bahundanda, Brahma's Hill, to the village at the top. As we crested the hill the first person to greet us was a laughing boy, who brought us to a tea shop in the tiny town square.

A young man at one of the tables jumped up and introduced himself as Ganesh. Evidently delighted to practice his English, he greeted me like a long lost cousin. He and his burly friend Eknath, both in their early twenties, brought me to the inn of a young Tibetan woman. She gave me a room across the narrow alley, at the top of a rickety ladder.

The streets bustled with activity. Vendors were heaping up doughnuts, corn on the cob, fried bread, hard boiled eggs, sweet cakes dripping with sugar. Ganesh pointed to the red string around his neck and to the yellow one his friend wore.

"Today is full moon," he said. "Full moon in August is Shiva's birthday. We change our necklace thread and our bracelet thread on Shiva's birthday. I am Brahman, my color is red. Eknath is Kshatriya, warrior caste; his color is yellow. Red, yellow—no problem. Eknath and I are best friends."

He put his arm around his friend, who smiled broadly.

Walking back through the square, Ganesh pointed out a shrine to Shiva under an enormous tree. An old woman was sweeping the ground before what looked like a cement box with a metal grate. I bowed *Namaste,* and peered into the box. All I could discern of the statue was that it was standing.

"This evening we break our fast," said Ganesh. "All the Hindu people have a good time today. We bring Shiva food and flowers, and we bring cow's milk. This is our offering. Then we take *tika* on our forehead."

"*Tika,* the red dot?" I asked. "What is it made from?"

"Dry colored flowers."

We had arrived at the brow of the hill, with unobstructed views to the north. Settlements crowned all the high hills, but none looked as large as Bahundanda.

"When we make the offering," said Ganesh, "and take *tika,* our sister-in-law gives us *janai,* the new thread. She weaves it for us, the colored thread. Red, yellow—no problem."

His friend beamed at his side.

"Everybody gives her money for this. She loves Shiva too. For women, red is for marriage; yellow, no problem. But my mother— my father is dead—she doesn't wear red."

The sun came through the clouds and lit up the landscape.

"Better she doesn't marry again. Only the crazy women do. I am with her. She doesn't need to marry. She wears black, green, yellow—no problem. But red she never wears."

I thought of the walled-off life of a woman in what seemed a basically sexist society, and her cast-off status after the man had gone.

"What about blue?" I said.

Ganesh shrugged and giggled. "The Tibetan at the foot of the hill—you passed his house—he says it is the color of the *dakini.* She is the sky walker. She lives on the top of the mountains, and she dances." He looked at his friend. "We don't know. That's what he says."

The festivities were gaining momentum. Little girls, all dressed up, ran in packs through the streets. The dust in the air turned gold in the setting sun. Some people began a rousing song made up, Ganesh said, from the names of Shiva.

"Names?" I said. "You mean, like different faces?"

Ganesh nodded enthusiastically.

"Are any of the faces female?"

He laughed uproariously, and clapped Eknath on the shoulder. "No, no female in the names. Only male."

Seeing my disappointment he patted my arm.

"Shiva is, we could say, the seed. Look!"—he pointed to a stand of bamboo by the inn—"can you see the seed in this? No, no seed. Bamboo is the Shakti. She is the life. She is the female. She is everything you see— you, me, those little girls. Shakti and Shiva, always together." He clasped his hands together. "Shiva is the seed you cannot see."

A gust of wind shook the bamboo.

Ganesh smiled and nodded. "Everything. You see?"

The concept reminded me of the *Shekinah* in Jerusalem: the spirit of all the people together, married to God in their prayers on the Shabbos.

Surrounded by villagers in the inn at night, I felt connected to people for the first time since I'd arrived. I bought some beer, and poured for everyone. We raised a toast. Mylar became the clown and danced something like a jig in the middle of the floor. A Tibetan monk started clapping his hands, and Mylar's leaps and spins grew more extravagant. The kids collapsed in laughter. A man by the stove started telling a story. Though I didn't know the words, I could read the expressions on his face and follow along.

I noticed the bottles were empty and rose to get more, but Ganesh held my arm.

"No, don't buy, unless you want. We have taken some just to join you. We do not drink."

I looked around at the glasses. All still full. Mine was the only one empty. The revelry I'd felt had come from the spirit in the people, not the beer.

The following morning Mylar and I set out at a good pace. The weather stayed with us. We reached Besisahar by nightfall, and set out at dawn with Lyla for Bhote Wodar. Constant walking had strengthened my legs. I struck out ahead at a fast pace. Crossing the stream outside Udipur, I lost my footing and crashed into the water with my pack. It was like watching a film in slow motion. I felt my elbow hit the jagged rock. Struggling to stand, I saw the blood gushing down my arm.

The blood made my adrenalin rise, and my actions precise. I pulled out my first-aid kit and doused the hole with peroxide. With a mirror I got a good look at my elbow: the gash was deep, but not to the bone. I felt a kinship with the chicken I'd eaten, whose raw flesh, sliced with the scimitar, resembled my own.

By the time Mylar arrived with Lyla, I had gotten a passable bandage in place, which he helped to tie. An hour later, in Bhote Wodar, the pharmacist examined my wound. A heavy-set man with glasses and a kindly face, he spoke halting English. He said I was lucky to have found him home; he was the only person within a day's walk who gave stitches. It was difficult to say how old he might be. Even with his thick magnifying glasses, he seemed to have trouble seeing.

In his opinion, the cut was not major. To my relief, since anaesthetics were non-existent, it would require no stitches. He sold me antibiotic powder to sprinkle in the wound, and enough gauze and tape to last until Kathmandu. For the rest of the descent to Dumre, I washed in the rivers and kept that arm out of the water.

Compared to the relative silence of the hills, the traffic in Kathmandu was overwhelming. The dust settled into my cut, which immediately got infected. I began changing the bandage three times a day and pouring in antibiotic powder, but the wound got larger. I noticed an English expatriate, whom I'd met before, hobbling along with an infected wound from the right knee down to the ankle, and shuddered at what could happen in the tropical city.

Searching for a trekking guide, I wanted three things: someone who knew the whole circuit and had done it at least once himself (I did not expect to find a female guide); who was strong enough to carry my pack as well as his own when we reached the nearly eighteen thousand foot pass of Thorung La; and who could speak English. I had very little money, but since it was still raining and not yet tourist season I hoped to find someone who would go for a cheaper price.

After several days I met Arjuna, a young man from the Gurkha tribe — the famed warriors who had fought in the British army — who agreed to go. He was much younger than I'd expected, but had already done the trek twice and was willing to start as soon as we were outfitted. A trekking store in the Thamel rented us the gear. At the last minute, however, Arjuna wanted to be paid in full for the entire twenty-one days or he would not go.

I said no one was paid in advance for a service they had not yet rendered. He said his parents were poor and needed the money to live while he was gone. We compromised on half in advance, the other half on completion. Kathmandu, I had already learned, was a city of wheeler dealers. I bought the bus tickets knowing that if he wanted, Arjuna had only to disappear. There was very little I could do.

But at dawn he was waving to me from the bus stop. We crossed the river that afternoon at Dumre and started up. The bush beans I'd noticed planted at the edges of the rice paddies had changed in the ten days since I'd last seen them. The bottom leaves were turning yellow. Fall, they said. The dry season was coming.

After two days walking, I found my companion almost as stubborn as I was. We disagreed on what hour to start: I did yoga before getting dressed; he wanted to strike out at dawn. What hour should we stop for lunch? Most Nepalis, he said, ate at eleven, but that was too early for me; I wanted to push on until noon. The last person he'd trekked with had been a German woman who had then become his lover. I said I had a lover I was satisfied with and was not looking for replacements. Unlike Eusebio in the Andes, he made me feel like an employer, and bridled at taking orders from a woman.

But he was the bridge I needed. He gave me phrases to memorize as we walked along. When someone passed, I would try them out: I am going to Manang. I write books. What is your work? I am heading over the Thorung La to Muktinath. Besides translating, Arjuna explained their reactions and added more phrases when needed: Yes, my hair is as short as my husband's. No, he is not here with me; he is working.

Great cumulus clouds sat at the edges of the sky, but did not rain. All the puddles in the road dried up in the tropical sun. We mopped ourselves as we walked along, and rested in the shade of enormous pipal trees—*Ficus religiosa,* the sacred fig tree. A stone wall was often found at its base, where a porter or passer-by could rest their burden, cool off, and admire the view. The great shade tree, pronounced "people" tree, was every walker's friend.

Arjuna said the pipal was sacred to Shiva and never cut down or uprooted. On every leaf, he said, one could see all the Hindu gods and goddesses dancing. Even if a seed got lodged in a crack and threatened to break down the wall of a house, the house would be allowed to fall apart, while the tree grew, protected. The Bodhi tree Buddha sat beneath when he became enlightened was a pipal. Both Hindus and Buddhists used the seeds for prayer beads.

Arjuna showed me how to quench my thirst with lemon, salt, and hot spices, instead of water. I observed him as we made our way in the broiling sun. About my height—tall by Nepalese standards—he carried himself with the steady untiring pace of a healthy twenty-four year old who was used to walking. He had dark eyes in a squarish face, with a sparse black beard he was letting grow. A bronzed complexion had already replaced his city pallor.

The air was shimmering over the ground as we approached Bhoti Wodar. Over the brow of a hill appeared the mountain that people had pointed to behind the clouds my last time there; the glacier stood in glorious contrast to the tropical valley at its feet.

"Look, Arjuna! Lam Jung Himal!"

Setting out early in the morning, I was surprised at the European couple taking the photo of a hotel owner on the edge of town. Except for three Yugoslavians who'd come racing past us with ski poles, there had been no Westerners trekking since we'd started. They were Danish, and bound like us for the Thorung La. They fell in line behind me as Arjuna led the way across the river. Since my fall I'd become very circumspect about rivers. I used my stick and crossed with great caution. At the bank I heard a splash, and turned around. The woman's face was covered with blood. Her husband was lifting her out of the water onto the bank on the other side.

I ran back. She'd fallen and hit her forehead on a rock. I spread out my first-aid kit and washed her face. Although not unconscious, she looked in shock. The gash above her eyebrow was wide and deep. Her husband, beside himself, kept patting her hand. I bandaged her head, and she asked for something to drink. He cradled her neck while she drank and the color returned to her face.

The woman was a nurse. She judged herself to have suffered a mild concussion, and wanted to see the gash for herself. My little mirror was not enough. I suggested we head back to the hotel where I had stayed, which had a large mirror in the dining room. After some minutes, she felt herself strong enough to walk. I gave Arjuna my pack to carry ahead; I'd catch up with him in the next town.

I shouldered her pack while her husband helped her stand. Slowly we made it back to my hotel. She was the calmest accident victim I had ever seen. Peering into the mirror we held above her, she agreed she would need stitches. We discussed the options. The three day trek back to Kathmandu was too long for a wound that size; she would probably never make it. She decided on the pharmacist I'd met in town.

We'd gathered a crowd by the time we reached his shop. I held her hand as she lay on the cot. The pharmacist tried to be gentle, but he was piercing living flesh with a large curved needle and no anaesthetic. As he poked the first hole through, she squeezed my hand and said nothing. Her husband ran for the street. The pharmacist tugged on the thick black thread. To my horror, he pulled it all the way through. The string had gone completely through her flesh and out again!

Dismayed, he pierced the flesh again, and again pulled the thread all the way through. It was like watching an S & M movie. His wife stepped up to his shoulder and spoke. She had him stop the next stitch in time, and tied the two ends together herself. Blood was flowing copiously from the wound. When he pierced the flesh and drew the thread all the way through again, it dawned on me that the man could not *see*. Even with his thick glasses, he was probably legally blind. He was doing it by feel.

I began talking quietly, as much for the woman and the pharmacist as myself.

"Easy does it now, easy... Not all the way, not— Okay, easy does it. Ah, that's nice, that's beautiful. Number two."

"How many more?" asked the woman. "I can't bear any more."

The gash, like an inverted L, needed at least one more stitch, at best two. But her iron grip was loosening. She was moving and wincing. The pharmacist pierced the skin again; pulling the black thread, he paused. I was sure he was doing it by feel. His wife stepped in to staunch the blood. He punctured the other side and stopped. His wife tied the two ends together and cut the thread.

"That's it," I said. "You're done."

The woman burst into tears. Her husband ran back in and grabbed her hand. The room was spinning around me. I ran out, sat in the road, and breathed deeply. We'd done it. Yes, we had. The gash looked like Frankenstein's, with three black strings, but it was closed. The pharmacist cleaned and bandaged her head, and I helped them back to the hotel.

"What's your name?" I asked.

We burst out laughing. They were Erica and Niels. I gauged them to be in their twenties. They debated going on anyway up to Manang and maybe over the pass, but I dissuaded them. The farther they walked from civilization, the more at risk they were. Her cut was too deep. They agreed to return to Kathmandu and see a doctor. They could always start again, or do part of the trek from the other side. They promised to leave me word in Kathmandu on where they were.

Heading out under the midday sun, I was Captain Careful crossing the river. I caught up with Arjuna by nightfall, outside Besisahar. Walking behind him alongside a ditch that cut through the village, I stopped amazed.

Fireflies were winking and swarming on the other side of the ditch. Where the Andean nights had had dozens, there were hundreds. Dipping and weaving in the velvety dark, the lights seemed to rearrange space and distance. The closest thing I'd ever seen to compare it to were the Northern Lights.

Day followed day and the road assumed all fealty, energy, and purpose. We became lean mean walking machines. Small thoughts were swallowed by the enormous landscape and open sky. The houses and villages perched over precipices and snuggled into hillsides were of a people I found modest and courageous. A recent earthquake in Kathmandu had reverberated up the valley, causing landslides and mud slides, destroying houses and downing bridges. In Ngadi, a mud slide had just buried two houses and killed five villagers. I could see where a chunk of the slope had simply slid off and fanned out as it came down, covering everything. White prayer flags fluttered like moths in the wind coming up the valley.

Walkers passing on the trail addressed each other in familial terms I began to understand: grandfather, father, daughter, son. Depending on the age of the speaker, I was older sister, younger sister, or sometimes mother. The custom created the sense of a common family streaming across the countryside.

In the absence of sexual activity, my senses reveled in the physical surroundings. The roaring of waterfalls and rivers; the thousand different smells of mud and moist vegetation; the roundness of rocks, clouds, hillsides, and slopes that curved like skirts swirling around a corner; the call of pleasure from a water buffalo, lolling in a muddy pool.

If, as Thoreau says, the walker owns everything she surveys, I especially owned the rivers. At the end of each day I sought out water to wash my clothes and the salt from my body. Wash in the river once, and it is yours, say the Nepalis. Going in, I belonged to the river, and the river to me; I didn't care that I had to stay clothed. I was the green and white flowing water, I was the flat rock to pound the clothes. The water was my private domain, a space without people, where I watched the bugs come out and darkness fall.

After more than a week of trekking and of following separate schedules, the distance between Arjuna and me as we hiked was getting wider. I'd explained at the beginning that we needn't be in each other's company all day; but if he walked ahead, he should stop at any possible danger and wait for me. If he chose to walk behind, and kept up his pace, he would probably never be more than fifteen minutes away.

But I was rarely seeing him except at meals, or in the town where we slept for the night. At a roadside inn in Jagat, I came upon a British surgeon who was walking as I was, with just a guide and very little baggage. While we waited for lunch, I watched his guide make sure his needs were attended to, and explained my problem.

He advised me to assert my desires more clearly. Since I was paying to have them met, I had a right to the services I required. Perhaps it had to do with my being a woman. He himself had had nothing but excellent service, and had not paid a cent in advance. It sounded so simple and civilized.

The next morning as I started out, Arjuna was eating a second breakfast. Since my best distance was made in the morning, I could not wait. An hour later, I was pushing up the gradual ascent on the east side of the Marsyangdi, across alpine terrain. The river gorge had widened and deepened. The view on the other side was fir woods, birch stands, and a long wonderful waterfall. It reminded me of the Colorado Rockies.

Suddenly the path fell away. A terrific landslide had wiped out everything. I had to traverse loose rubble that stretched hundreds of feet above me, and hundreds of feet down to the river. The scale was awesome. The purchase I had on the makeshift detour was no slimmer than on parts of the trail I had already covered, but as I picked my way along I began to wonder about the likelihood of one of the boulders above me rolling down. If I slipped, would I tumble directly down to the water, or catch myself midway? Everything was so loose, a minor stumble could dislodge the slope in a roaring second.

Within minutes I was frozen with fear. Reaching a bend in the slope, I did not have the confidence to hop around it. I was stuck. The scree above me was a grim towering presence; the scree below a slide to certain death. I would have to wait for Arjuna. I sat down and took out my notebook. After an hour I was still waiting. The fear in the pit of my stomach had turned to anger, but it could not take me around the bend.

When Arjuna came into view atop the landslide, he was startled to see me.

"What are you doing here?" he whispered. "This is not a place to sit. Let's move away quickly."

He held my hand around the far side of the curve and across the steeper incline that followed until the land resumed—whole, unscarred, and relatively level—on the other side. He let go of my hand.

"Sitting in such a place is dangerous," he said matter-of-factly.

I threw down my walking stick and my pack as well.

"Do you think I had a choice?! Do you think I stayed because I liked the view?!"

I was hopping up and down, shouting and punching the air.

"I was stuck, you idiot! Trapped! I couldn't move forward or backward! If you had been anywhere nearer, like we said, I wouldn't have had to wait a whole hour watching those boulders about to roll!"

His eyes had grown wide. A bird screeched from somewhere up the trail. I leaned against a rock and looked away. As though we had just watched a bear bound across the trail and over the edge, leaving a calm sheltered world in her wake, a small breeze reached us, the water below sparkled green in the sun. I explained what I felt our agreement was, and asked what he thought. He agreed we should not travel so far apart. We shared some water. Shouldering our packs again, we set out.

The autumnal smells and sounds of Bagarchap reminded me of home: wood smoke, ripe apples, the tang in the air before a killing frost, axes ringing against the wood, and the murmur of water. An intricate maze of canals ran under the streets and outhouses of the mountain town.

My bathing in the rivers and streams was finished. I asked the innkeeper for a pail of hot water, and she gave me a sheltered place behind the inn to wash. A welcome sun turned the backyard golden, with its newly harvested squashes and gourds, its baskets of apples, its yellow leaves.

In the last of the afternoon, I sat with a hydroelectric engineer at a table in front of the inn. He was a chunky little man—in his forties, I guessed—whose eyes darted about with ceaseless interest at everything around us. He had just come from Pisang, two days up the trail.

His job was to seek out small, practicable hydroelectric sites as possible government projects—to provide local villagers with the power they needed without resorting to the dwindling forests. He envisioned future generations inhabiting a much bleaker terrain, with denuded slopes and eroded farmland, and spoke of his work with a certain urgency.

I asked him about Shiva and Shakti, and about female deities. Judging by his face, I seemed to have struck a happy chord.

"Ah," he said, leaning back in his seat, "you see, unlike your Christianity, we account for all the energies, positive and negative. Nothing is forbidden, everything has its place. Each of the gods and goddesses contains a particular energy—the same energy we contain, you and I—but in its pure form. Take Kali, for instance, the consort of Shiva. Now we are all part of Shiva, the one we call Lord of All, rather like the one you Christians call God."

"I'm not Christian."

"Oh, well, anyway—"

"I thought his consort was Shakti. Is Shiva the male everyone marries?"

"In the sense that anything at that level is male or female. Shiva is consciousness, you see, everything that exists—the power that keeps everything in existence and moving along, destroying and regenerating. But Kali, the female side, is the one you see working.

"She is the one who destroys so rebirth can occur, so things can change. Have you heard people speak of the look of Kali? When a person's anger is strong and comes out raging, we see it as a form of Kali and back away. We have great respect for that anger. Haven't you ever seen a woman give that look?"

"Not really. All the women I've encountered seem to be rather submissive. But I guess you mean anger in men, too."

"The point is, the woman is not Kali and not pretending to be Kali. But the energy she is part of is of that goddess. In other words, within us are the seeds of all the gods and goddesses we seek."

He turned his gaze from the far hills to the table.

"You see, we take ourselves much less seriously than you Westerners do. When we bring an offering to the gods, we are honoring them outside and inside ourselves."

He was tapping his outstretched fingers together judiciously over the table.

"And, since we believe in reincarnation and the Law of Karma, we take responsibility for everything that comes to us apparently at random from the universe. The system is totally just. Why fight it? What comes is exactly what we need to experience, for whomever we are to become."

"So then our sitting here and talking, you and I," I said, "and watching that bit of sun, was also arranged."

He flashed a wide smile, showing the gold tooth behind his incisor.

"Exactly."

The following morning the weather set in cold and wet. After the tropics and alpine slopes, we were heading into temperate forests much like the forests of New York State. Perhaps because I assumed Arjuna would dawdle over breakfast, I'd been rather brusque with him, and he'd turned away looking hurt. On the trail I thought about it.

Often my impatience had an imperious edge that brooked no opposition. My rage, aimed against myself or anyone else, could be crippling and unrelenting. Gods and goddesses running through oneself notwithstanding, I felt I needed to be kinder to others, and kinder to myself. On the wet ground of the forest floor I found a six inch piece of bright red yarn, like the wool I'd collected in the Cordillera Blanca for my rattle. I looped it around my ring finger as a reminder.

Walking through woods so similar to the Catskills, where I'd hiked for years, I felt an animal sense of belonging. The sudden curtailment of visible distance brought my focus down to the shapes of puddles, the hue of the earth under certain trees, the prevailing vegetation. I recognized birch, pine, spruce and oak trees; wild asters, goldenrod, yarrow, and a particularly brutal strain of stinging nettles.

But after hours of the damp cold seeping in, despite my pace, I tried to detach myself by imagining warmer scenes. I pictured myself on a raw day walking out of the woods up to my house, and opening the door to the rush of warmth from the wood stove. Around me the Marsyangdi Valley narrowed to a gorge. The woods got darker, the rain increased.

I calculated the hour—it would be nighttime at my house— and imagined myself entering and putting the small light on in the kitchen. I stood at the pantry shelves and chose my tea: Lobsang Suchong. I loved the smell. When the kettle whistled, I filled my cup and let the tea steep. I added honey and milk. To make each detail come alive took enormous concentration. At last I sat at the kitchen table. It was quiet. The friends staying at my house were asleep. I drank my tea.

The visualization kept me warm and busy as I slogged along. By the time I drank the tea in my kitchen, two hours had passed and I'd covered four miles up the increasingly narrow river gorge. The engineer in Bagarchap was right. I'd seen whole tracts of forests cleared, and much new building, but nothing planted.

At a clearing draped in mist was a Buddhist temple, newly built of stone and raw wood, with a pine bough set athwart the entrance. I assumed it meant no one was in and visitors were unwelcome. I arranged my coverings to rest in the rain. Atop my black rubber rain poncho I had a white voluminous plastic sheet with arm holes and a hood. Together I could make them stand around me like a portable lean-to.

Out of the fog came an old man I'd been crossing paths with since the morning. In his ill-fitting overcoat and shredded sneakers he could have stepped out of a Kurosawa movie. Though he looked about seventy, with his matted gray hair and sparse beard over weathered Tibetan features, he had the inexorable pace of a much younger person. Something about his eyes made me think of a pilgrim bound urgently for some mecca in the distance.

Hours before, he'd preceded me up a series of steep switchbacks. Reaching the top, he'd done something I'd always wanted to do. He threw himself back onto a large rock, like a sacrifice for carrion birds, and aimed a lamentation loud with reproach, complaint, and indignation at the sky. It echoed how I felt exactly. Then, just as suddenly, he jumped up and scurried on.

As he hurried past my makeshift tent, I realized I'd spoken to no one all day. The old man neither looked up nor waved. I wanted to ask him where he was going. "Are you going to Manang?" That was one of my phrases. By the time I formed the words in my mind, he was halfway across the field.

I shouldered my pack and lit out after him, but he was fast. I got to within fifty yards—almost close enough to shout—when he jumped off the path and scuttled up a nearby hill. As my friend in Bagarchap would say, I was meant to never know where he was going.

Out on the grassy flats Arjuna caught up, and we walked together. We had reached the plain of Manang, or Tibetan Plateau, a shelf running east-west between two mountain ranges of the

Himalayas, and the top part of the twenty-one day loop around the Annapurnas. From the ten thousand foot elevation we would gain only fifteen hundred feet a day until we reached Thorung Phedi, the foot of the pass. Around us herds of horses grazed among the stands of spruce and pine.

The guidebook recommended spending several days in the town of Manang, one day up the trail, to get accustomed to the altitude before attempting to cross the Thorung La, the 17,700 foot pass. In the dreary weather the pass began to loom enormous and unfriendly. The clouds had withdrawn to the feet of the Annapurnas, hidden from view to our left. A steady cold wind had replaced the rain. I was chilled to the bone.

Ba was the Napalese word for people. The *Manang-ba* had been the real traders throughout the Himalayas until 1960, when the Chinese had taken over Tibet and closed the borders. A host of white prayer flags fluttered from the flat roofs in Pisang, our town for the night. None of the stone inns we passed seemed to promise much warmth.

A man approached on horseback. His hair and moustache were jet black; his skin was leathery from exposure. I had seen a photo once, in the *Family of Man* exhibition, of a horseman (or horsewoman, it was difficult to tell) in the Kirghiz Republic of Russia, riding full tilt down a mountain. In his (or her) face was an expression of wild delight that reminded me of the man before us. He was glorious.

"Looking for something? I have it right here."

His body language as he dismounted was direct and uncomplicated. I was amazed at his English. He led us to a stone inn, two stories high, with tall windows. Arjuna picked a room on the second floor near the stairwell. The man showed me a narrow room with one drafty window overlooking the Marsyangdi. In the dim interior, he pounded the only article of furniture, a straw mattress on a wooden plank.

"Very good bed."

I could see he was used to pursuing women, and used to winning. My mind jumped ahead to the night. I could leave the door unlocked if I wished; it was as simple as that.

"You want *chai*? Hot water for wash?"

I nodded and smiled at him.

In the kitchen was a plain woman of indeterminate age, who could have been his housekeeper, his sister, or his aunt. She had large protruding teeth when she smiled. She gave Arjuna and me tiny stools by the door of the stove, to warm ourselves while she heated the water.

Early in the trek Arjuna had explained how Nepalis considered visitors. God is the guest, the guest is God, was how they put it. All actions for personal benefit were dropped before the service due a guest until the guest was satisfied.

We had begun to run into some trekking parties. Mainly Europeans, they usually sat together at a table, while their porters and guides gathered around the stove. As the stove was where I wanted to be, Arjuna's service as interpreter was invaluable. I was understanding more of the customs and language every day.

The horseman had disappeared. The woman said with our meal of *daal baat* we would have a special treat of fresh peas and potatoes. A young woman she introduced as her daughter arrived in time to have tea with us. She handed me a glass of *rakshi*. I had never had *rakshi* before. The deceptively tasty homemade liquor packed a mean wallop. After one glass I was warmed up, ready for a stroll before dinner. I lit out for the fields beyond the bridge. Climbing to a stone wall halfway up the slope, I surveyed the whole valley.

The fields covered with recently cut buckwheat and barley, pink and green, looked like a tapestry. The checkerboard pattern reminded me of one design on neolithic pottery, where all the decorative symbols represented the Goddess. That net design was her moisture and fertility. I thought of the horseman, who was exactly the type I was drawn to. I loved the woman I was who liked men, for companionship, and for the fun and pleasure. Whatever goddess that was, as the man in Bagarchap would have it, I saluted her in myself.

I returned to the inn. A young man was cooking in the kitchen. I took my stool next to Arjuna. The woman entered with a basket of peas for us to shell. I had not been asked to help with a meal since I'd been in Nepal; the gesture made me feel like part of the family. A little girl of about five came in and sat next to the woman—another daughter, I thought.

The horseman ducked through the doorway, and took the seat covered with a sheepskin in the corner nook next to the stove. It was clearly his place. He eyed me briefly. The woman poured him a glass of *rakshi*. Then she got up from her place and went over and sat next to him, and he asked her something. When she turned to him, her eyes were shining. This was not his housekeeper; it was his woman. She was in love with him, her eyes said so. I realized the daughter I'd met that afternoon resembled him, and the little girl as well.

So, after the birth of their first child, he'd probably taken off, and the woman had kept the inn and run the business. For the next ten to fifteen years, he'd run after every skirt in the province of Manang, fathered a mess of kids, and the woman had waited. Then he'd come back and they'd had a second daughter. That's how I saw it, watching them over my second glass of *rakshi*.

Through the shelling of peas there was a good deal of banter, of which I understood nothing except my inclusion in the circle of laughter—familial friendly laughter. The howling wind made the kitchen seem small and protected. After our banquet, Arjuna and the young cook went to bed. There were just the three of us. The little girl slept in her mother's lap.

I constructed a version of "Thank you for letting me into your family," and hoped they understood.

As I stood up to go, the horseman winked.

"I'll bring you up your tea to your room."

I shook my head.

"No, thank you. Enough tea. Tomorrow."

His eyebrows went up in surprise. I rubbed the red string on my finger. I was that woman at the stove. I had been that woman, and I was her now. Nothing in the world could make me hurt her.

We were going at a good pace across the plain. Between the villages were herds of yaks and the short muscular horses of the Manang-ba. The sober landscape of dry grass and gray sky was relieved from time to time by clumps of rosebushes in autumnal color. They bore bright red rose hips, the size of tiny tomatoes. I shared one stand with a white baby yak, who made sure the sprawling branches stayed between us as we gobbled the fruit on separate sides of the bush.

At twelve thousand feet we stayed the night in the town of Manang, which took in all the trekkers en route to the pass. Rising the next morning at dawn, I saw the veils of mist lift across the valley, revealing a frozen lake, and Annapurna III and Gangapurna in their entirety. Annapurna was the Goddess of Food. Since more water came from the glaciers to feed the crops on the plain than fell from the sky, the Annapurnas were aptly named. The peaks that had been hidden by clouds were wildly beautiful, majestic, and serene. We decided, despite the guidebook, to push on.

At five in the afternoon, Arjuna and I reached Lattar at fourteen thousand feet—a falling down hut in the rain. No one was home. I had never considered that possibility. We carried some packaged food to eat for sustenance, but without a tent or a fire we could look foward to a pretty bleak night. By luck, the front door was unlocked. In the small courtyard was a battered table and sodden clumps of animal skins sitting in the rain.

Of the four doors off the courtyard, two were open. The rain increased. I chose the room with the least amount of water coming through the roof. Night was falling. Finding my way by flashlight in the windowless chamber, I strung up my white plastic cape, hooking it to sticks in the thatched roof, which looked like it had never been dry. Mushrooms were growing from the ceiling.

Above the damp plank that would be my bed, I angled the plastic so the water would run off some feet away. For good measure, I stood an open umbrella over my pack. I rolled out my thin pad onto the bench and laid my sleeping bag on top. The rain on my canopy began a steady tattoo. I stepped back and surveyed what I felt was a very passable bivouac.

After dark the owner of the hut arrived: a yak herder in his thirties, with the same wild beauty as the horseman in Pisang. He was very gracious about our having let ourselves in. In the kitchen he quickly made a fire, and threw in an offering of yak butter. Then he made tea with fresh yak milk for himself, Arjuna, and me.

In Arjuna's face I read consternation, and wondered why. The tea was sweet and the warmth a godsend. I watched the herdsman prepare a meal of boiled potatoes and thought how lonely his life must be, day after day in the bleak terrain. When I asked him, through Arjuna, if he liked his life out there, he shrugged. He seemed to think it a nonsensical question. It wasn't a matter of like or dislike; it was his life.

I went to sleep with the sound of his humming about the house. In the morning he had already gone. His son, a beautiful boy of about ten, was making our breakfast. I headed down to the rivulet and ducked behind some rocks to wash. The facing slope was covered with snow, the sky was gray. I squatted on the muddy bank and brushed my teeth with the icy water. The vast grim tracts brought a dull apprehension; the pass was looming larger every second. I took out my tiny pocket mirror, and looked at my face.

Smoke filled the kitchen from the young boy's fire. He served Tibetan flat bread with jam, and strong tea with yak milk. Arjuna and I drank copious amounts, while the boy, curious and shy, watched quietly.

He rummaged through a pile of rags in the cupboard behind him; to my surprise, he came out with an oval hand mirror. When

Arjuna and I discussed the trail ahead, in English, the boy held the mirror before him and chattered to himself. He was like some lonely prince of an ancient race, free of all constraints but the forbidding landscape.

We set out in late morning for the inn at Thorung Phedi, the foot of the pass. We would only be climbing a thousand feet, and advancing perhaps three miles. It was our last day of grace before the pass. As we walked, I took more and more rest stops. My heartbeat seemed to fill my whole body. All conversations took place from a sitting position; I didn't have enough breath to walk and talk at once.

I asked Arjuna what had bothered him the night before.

"You remember I explained how we say God is the guest?"

I nodded.

"When the yak herder made the tea, he made it for himself as well, and was already drinking when he gave us ours." He shook his head. "That is not the way things are done."

I was nonplused. All the conditions of the night and morning—the leaking roof, his wet sleeping bag, the added weight in his pack of the heavy items I could no longer carry—none of this bothered Arjuna. But a countryman who carried himself incorrectly seemed to threaten the equilibrium of the universe. He could neither accept nor overlook it.

Making my way at a snail's pace, I had ample time to look around at the bleak relentless terrain. A bird with a golden underbelly flew over us again and again as we dragged ourselves through the drizzle. It reminded me of the ácaca in the Andes, and I missed the raucous cackle.

It was mid-afternoon when Arjuna pointed up the stony slope to a dark pile of rocks at the edge. I could vaguely discern the outlines of a building. The inn at Thorung Phedi. As we approached, a youngish looking man standing on the edge called out in greeting. He was looking off under his hand at the path we had covered.

I turned around. Nothing there. I asked what he saw. He sighed and said he also saw nothing. He was waiting for a friend who might be coming. His face was outlined against the rocky slope. I thought, if the yak herder's life had been lonely, this man's life must be doubly so. He showed me his garden protected by a stone wall, where he had some hardy spinach, potatoes, and cabbage growing. I'd been told that sometimes the inn was closed. I was infinitely grateful he had taken it over, and planted the food and gathered the brush for kindling.

Just before dark, a large group arrived. A French couple, a single Israeli, and a trio of Germans, with their respective porters—four in all. The innkeeper was quietly busy at the stove. The *daal baat* would take an hour and a half. He was also making an extra treat of potatoes and onions. I sat at the stove, drying my socks and gloves on my knees. Next to me was Arjuna, and around us, at varying distances from the stove, the other porters.

One lantern sat on the table against the wall, where the new group sat and waited; the other shone on the innkeeper and his pots and pans. From time to time he added a precious stick of wood to the fire.

"How long before the food is ready? We are very hungry!"

The tone of voice made me cringe. The Israeli addressed the man at the stove, who nodded and said nothing. The people began to talk among themselves, as hikers will, about how hungry they were, how much they could eat, and what dishes they would like to have, down to the tiniest details.

Suddenly the door flew open and a man entered, wrapped in what looked like a heavy bathrobe. On his thick black hair was an inch of snow. He greeted the innkeeper, and took a place on the bench behind the stove. Arjuna explained he had just come down from the pass.

"In the dark?!!" I said.

It was more an expression of wonder than a question.

Arjuna translated. The man did not seem to think his act particularly noteworthy. He said the weather had not been good. As far as I was concerned, he was a hero.

The food was ready. The innkeeper served the group at the table, Arjuna and me. Only then was there room on the stove to boil water. He made a pot of tea and served the newcomer, the porters, and lastly, himself.

"Not eating?" I asked, indicating the man in the bathrobe.

"We aren't hungry yet," said the innkeeper.

The people at the table were as good as their word. After the first helping they asked for seconds. I watched the innkeeper spoon out the last of the peas and rice. He would have to cook a whole new batch for the porters, the newcomer, and himself. He carefully scooped out the potatoes and onions to save for the second sitting. One of the German boys came over, and pointed.

"I'll have the rest of those potatoes," he said.

"Wait," I said. "There are no more left. He's saving those for the people who haven't eaten yet."

The young man looked at me as though I were crazy, and held out his plate. The innkeeper dropped in a small portion and covered the rest.

The Frenchwoman called out in a loud voice for apple pancakes, as though addressing a waiter in a crowded cafe.

I looked at her across the room. "There's only so much room on the stove, you know. These people won't even begin to cook for themselves until you're done eating."

"My money is good. I'm entitled to ask for pancakes."

Entitled. I felt like telling her she should get down on her knees and thank God someone was here at the pass so she wouldn't have to starve in the snow, but I said nothing. The newcomer was quietly drinking his tea and drying his head with a rag.

"That's why we cannot allow ourselves to do it your way," Arjuna murmured. "One time selfish, there is never an end."

I woke up at five and crept outside to check the weather. A fine sleet was driving down. The innkeeper came out behind me, looked up the trail angling off to the right, and said it did not look too good. The wind was moving the sleet horizontally across the slope. A quarter mile up, the trail was socked in. The Germans came out and declared it quite unsuitable for crossing the pass, which suited me fine. I was going.

The innkeeper made us hot breakfast. Readying our packs outside, Arjuna pointed out a herd of wild sheep, almost invisible in the gray and brown terrain, making their way single file along a wrinkle in the rock face. They were coming down for water or fleeing the bad weather up above.

A gray bird flew past us and landed on the trail. He started hopping uphill and it seemed a signal for us to get moving. I had carried the pass like an ominous presence for almost two weeks. I wanted to go, if for no other reason than to get it over with.

The altitude differential from Thorung Phedi to the pass at Thorung La was three thousand, three hundred feet—not an earthshaking amount; I'd done twice that in a long afternoon. It was the oxygen loss. The highest I'd ever been in the Andes was almost two thousand feet lower.

In the next four hours I prayed to every deity I had ever known, in every language, as I toiled uphill. Poor Arjuna. I kept heading toward stones to rest, like a recalcitrant burro, and he coaxed me onward again and again.

I thought of the substances I wished I had to help me. In the Andes I'd chewed coca leaves, taken Coramine, the respiratory stimulant, and electrolytes to replace the ones I'd lost. But what really had gotten me to the top was perseverance: a dogged will and leg muscles that kept hauling me up, no matter what. I thought of an herb seller in Cuzco who'd given me tiny peppery seeds she'd sworn would help me climb, and they had. My mouth had burned so fiercely I'd forgotten to think about my heart.

That was the other part: to engage the mind so the body could do its job. I had the prayers and poems I recited to myself, the water, my legs, and Arjuna prying me off the rocks and urging me on. My eyes were beating. My head, my ears, my lips, my heart, my lungs, my hands—everything was beating. I was a giant walking heartbeat.

Looking up from the ground, I could not discern the brim of my cap from the gray of the landscape. It all blended together. Arjuna was the soul of patience. Relentlessly we pushed on. The sleet pulled off and fell again as snow.

We reached the top of a hill, a flat place between two walls of granite, and came upon a makeshift cairn. The pile of rocks, twelve feet high, bristled with prayer flags, ribbons, shredded plastic banners, tin cans, coins, and hiking insignia. It was a wonderful home-made shrine.

This was it, the Thorung La! I couldn't believe our good fortune. I sat down in the rubble beside the cairn. Arjuna got out the camera and took my picture. I took his. We shared a candy bar, and joked about the bizarre outfits we were wearing, made up of our entire respective wardrobes.

Suddenly everything closed in. The world became small and dense and white. Arjuna looked faintly green.

"It's a white out," he said.

He tilted his head back and drank from the canteen. An avalanche roared behind him. Then another. In our reduced circumference it was difficult to ascertain their distance from us. Another one sounded, slightly nearer. A roar, and then a plop at the end.

"Do you think we'll die out here?"

Arjuna didn't answer. He was scurrying about, trying to find the trail. The snow had obliterated any traces on the ground. The fog made it impossible to read the contours of the land and approximate a way out.

I pictured the mountains on either side as two fierce deities, Khatung Kang and Yakawa Kang, jealously guarding their domain. What was I doing there? The upper regions of the earth did not belong to human beings, but to others who did not welcome strangers. They were meant to be crossed over quickly, with respect.

An avalanche sounded close by. I started, then slumped back against the cairn. If this was it, it was it. Nothing I could do about it. I grinned at the thought that the only entitlement I could claim to being there was that I was there. I had arrived on my own two feet, and maybe that counted for something.

Khatung Kang and Yakawa Kang. I *namaste*'d to them in my mind. And the blue skinned *dakini,* who danced on the top of mountains. May her power over the place remain absolute. I was only passing through.

Arjuna's voice came through the whiteness.

"I found it!"

The fog withdrew as we cut a course through the middle of a wide valley; then the trail dipped sharply down. If the ascent had been rock and moraine, the current terrain was mud. Mud and more mud, going straight down. But as we lost elevation, great energy returned. I felt I could slide down rivers of mud, thousands of feet of unremitting mud, if with every breath I sucked in, I got stronger.

We reached Muktinath in the late afternoon. Above the town was a grove of poplars; even in the rain their leaves were dancing. Legend said Padmasambhava, who brought Buddhism from India to Tibet, had stopped en route and meditated in Muktinath. Eighty-four *siddhas*—powerful male and female saint-magicians— had also passed through on their way to Tibet and left behind their walking sticks, which had turned into poplar trees.

In the Hindu epic Mahabharata, Muktinath was called Shaligrama, because of the shaligrams, the ammonite fossils found in the area. One hundred and fifty million years old, the small black segmented spirals were sacred to the Hindus as representing Vishnu, and to the Buddhists as Gawa Jopta, the serpent deity. I bought one from a woman near the village well.

The Hindus said Brahma had consecrated Muktinath by lighting a fire on top of water and another on top of stone, which were said to be still burning. Arjuna and I visited the temple the following morning. The woman did not question if I was a Hindu or a Buddhist. She simply let us in.

The river water had been channeled into spouts shaped like animal heads, and ran down the temple walls in manmade cascades. There was a large blackened circle in the dust of the courtyard from a recent fire. I imagined some ceremony in the dark, accompanied by the splashing water.

The woman brought us into the shrine room. On a platform three feet off the ground was an enormous Buddha with an ecstatic face. Was it Padmasambhava? Sakyamuni? The woman drew aside the brocaded cloth of the platform. Directly under the Buddha was a spring of water, on which a fire was burning; on the right another fire burned on a stone. Fire on water, fire on stone: I could understand the holiness of that.

The woman let the cloth fall back. She was young and modest. Her hair was hidden under a scarf, showing her ears.

"What is the Buddha's name?" I asked.

"Vishnu."

Vishnu was a Hindu god, the principle of cohesion, light, and truth. Buddha was thought to be an incarnation of Vishnu. Did it matter what anyone was called? Everything intertwined. Khatung Kang and Yakawa Kang were never far away. I imagined shamanic drums and rattles blending their sound with the water as the fire blazed. We left some rupees for the temple in a box by the door.

The line of peaks, hidden the night before, came into view: Tukuche, Daulagiri, and Tilicho Peak. We were striding westward down the long valley of the Jhong Khola. It joined the Kali Gandaki river and a whole new river valley at the town of Kagbeni. Behind us to the east, the saddle of the Thorung La was brilliantly white against a clear blue sky. Whoever was crossing that day had perfect weather.

We were overtaken on the trail by six soldiers walking from one barracks to another. I fell in step beside one of them, a goodlooking young man with wonderful teeth. As we followed each other over walls, across streams, keeping to the verges of rocky paths, hopping from stone to stone in the mud, we bantered in our small store of the other's language.

After half an hour he asked how old I was. I said I was forty-six, and returned the question. He said he was thirty, and that, in his opinion, there was really not much difference between thirty and forty. He didn't look a day over twenty-two, but I was delighted that he wanted to. The bellwether we had been hearing caught up and passed us, leading his line of a hundred sheep, three shepherds, and two small dogs. In Jharkot, the soldiers left us.

The *chorten* at the village entrance was typical of the ones we'd been passing. A row of cannisters on spindles stood on a long stone wall surmounted by a roof. In the cannisters, or prayer wheels, were sacred scrolls. Keeping the *chorten* on the right, you spun the row of cannisters with the right hand, thus setting the prayers into motion.

I loved spinning the whole row of them, and while my mind was engaged in the next moment—the cedar branches in the town square, the light and shadow beneath its branches—the prayer wheels would still be going. Moving ahead, I was simultaneously staying behind and praying.

We reached Kagbeni in the afternoon. *Kag* means blockade, and *beni* means joining of rivers. The hiking manual said river junctions were sacred to the local people. Before Nepal was a unified nation, the king who'd sat in the fortress town had controlled and taxed the grain that came up from the south, and the wool and salt that came down from Tibet. Trails went out from the town to the four directions. Another name for the Kali Gandaki river was the *Thak Khola,* the customs river.

Entering the town was like penetrating an intricate padlock. Every inch of space was utilized. Houses and stables and cobbled alleys were interlocked with the village well, stone tunnels, granaries and walled inns. Our innkeeper, a Tibetan woman in a brown dress and native apron, gave me a room on the second floor that had a door to the roof. I had a clear view over the roofs of the town, up to the Thorung La.

I walked down to the wall overlooking the Kali Gandaki river; it ran through the deepest defile on earth. The afternoon sun on the surface of the water turned it into a light blue road heading north to Mustang, the fabled kingdom of Lo, and beyond, to Tibet. Behind me was the Thorung La. Across the river was a trail cutting sharply up the slope on which a line of goats was descending. Their bells came intermittently as I turned in place. North, east, south, west. I was standing at the center of an ancient crossroads.

Someone came and stood beside me. It was a man in his late twenties, who greeted me in English. I asked what my chances were of walking north through Mustang to Tibet. I knew entrance was forbidden to outsiders, but I could see the trail along the river. What was to stop me from taking it?

He shook his head. I might get a day's journey in, he said, but soldiers would stop me sooner or later. Mustang was the wild province. The people did not recognize themselves as being under the Nepalese government, so the government wanted no strangers there. Moreover, since it bordered Tibet, the Chinese did not welcome visitors either.

When I expressed regret, he smiled benignly.

"Another time you'll return. Let me show you something."

He brought me to the northern entrance to the town. Set into the wall was a terra cotta statue of a male deity.

"We also have our border guards. He protects our town."

I nodded, but was not enthusiastic.

"Since the rivers cross here, I would have thought she would be female."

"Ah," he said, and led me down to the southern entrance. Set into the wall at ground level was a female deity, much smaller than the male. Her head was dark with the oil of hands that had touched her in passing.

"Both," said the man. "We must have both."

Nilgiri, to the south, was dazzling in sunset colors.

I got a pail from the inn to wash my clothes. Shepherds herded their animals through the stone archway and across the square as I watched from the well. The tinkling bells and clopping hooves on the cobblestones gave to the everyday ordinary act the solemnity of ritual.

From my rooftop I watched the goats nestle together in the walled inner courtyard below. A caravan of donkeys with their cowbells and hollow kettle sounds had arrived from somewhere and were headed for sleep. The moon rose full and round over the Thorung La.

In the dining room of the inn, a man who looked Tibetan ordered more *chang,* the homemade beer. He was tall and thin, with graying strands in his hair, and looked like a cross between a merchant and a pilgrim. After my own glass of *chang,* I tried out my Nelapese. Arjuna watched, amused, and would not translate.

"Do you live in a house? Is it big? Do you have a dog? I am a writer. What is your work? Do you have a cat?"

The man said, if I understood correctly, that he lived in a small house by a small river. He had a dog and some sheep. He did not have a cat.

"Do you speak Nepalese in your house?"

No, he spoke the language of Mustang, the same as the Chinese across the river.

"The Chinese across the river?!" He meant Tibet. "What is the other side like? What is their work?"

A great map of crinkles formed at his eyes as he laughed. "The other side looks like my side. They too have sheep."

I woke to the moon streaming through my window. It was midnight. I had just had a dream.

I was informed by someone I could not see that I would be marrying Shiva. I was told to get ready and prepare for the wedding. It was an unusual event for a Westerner, they said. I looked down at what I was wearing—the same blue cotton skirt, the same light blue T-shirt, and my boots. I said I couldn't do it. I had nothing to wear. I had no wedding clothes, only hiking gear.

They advised me to weave a necklace of flowers, yellow flowers. I should wash in the river, and cover my body with scented oil. It didn't matter what else I wore. The instructions were specific; I went to carry them out at once. Preparations were going on around me when I woke up.

I opened the door to the roof and stepped out. The rooftops below and the mountains on all sides were blue white under the moon. A small wind ruffled my clothes on the line. It brought the smell of wood smoke and water, perhaps the river. I fiddled with the string on my left hand and felt like crying. It was a wonderful dream.

In the morning Arjuna's muffled voice called through his door: he'd be along shortly, I shouldn't wait. I headed out, following the trail from Kagbeni southward. Nilgiri blazed in the morning sun and filled the horizon. Deeper than the Grand Canyon, the great new river valley widened, clear and crisp with the feel of fall. It was perfect weather for walking.

I stretched out on the flat terrain and covered several miles before the path angled up the cliff face to my left. In fact, there were several paths. I took the one that seemed the most likely. But after twenty minutes, when the grade got steeper and the path veered closer to the edge, I began to get worried.

The trail narrowed. No footprints, no broken twigs. The evidence of other hikers disappeared. I could see the river five hundred feet or more straight down, and found myself leaning into the hillside away from the brink. I stumbled on a pebble and caught myself up so sharply my heart was in my mouth. I hadn't realized how tense I was until I sat down on a rock. My hands were shaking.

From my vantage point I could appreciate just how steep the incline had been, how high I'd climbed, and how dangerous backtracking would be with the drop always in sight. I decided I did not want to go on. Why should I think it would get any better up ahead? I suddenly heard the words of Aneek, the woman mountain climber in Kathmandu:

"The time to be careful is after you've reached the pass. Once people reach their objective, they tend to get careless. Most accidents happen on the way down."

I had a clear view of the shoreline I had walked from Kagbeni. As I watched, three hikers approached and turned in where the paths ascended. Their steady progress up another trail confirmed my suspicions. I'd taken the wrong one. I stood up, gauging my choices: ahead was twenty feet of loose scree, with a barely discernible suggestion of a trail; behind me was the drop. I sat back down.

A young Nepali, a man in his twenties, came up the trail with a hopping gait. Clearly in his element, he reminded me of a friend in Peru I used to watch do the same thing—run on the edge. It had always seemed to me like he was deliberately flirting with death, but he'd sworn it wasn't that at all.

"When I'm in danger, I dance," he'd said.

By that he meant, I thought, that he didn't look down or tense his muscles or hold himself back. He simply relaxed and allowed his body to do what he knew how to do. He gave in, and danced with the earth.

The man came abreast of me on my rock.

"I can't move," I said. "I can't go up or down."

He did not break stride as he looked at me, and passed. "Then you shouldn't be here."

He skipped onto the loose scree, and in eight strides made it to the other side. I pictured myself following suit, and in the middle starting to slide, then grabbing for a foothold as I shot out over the edge. He was right. I shouldn't be there.

Finally Arjuna came into view on the shoreline and angled uphill. I called to him and waved my hat. He beckoned me over to where he was. I beckoned him up in reply. We kept it up for several minutes, each one waving the other over, until I got frantic. Suppose he went on, suppose he left me. I shook my stick wildly—up the hill, down the hill, over the edge. I was trying to communicate that I couldn't move.

At last he started up. When he got within shouting distance, he asked why I didn't walk down the trail. I told him down looked harder than up, I was too close to the edge, and I didn't want to die.

He climbed to where I was and held out his hand.

"Hold my hand. I'll walk you down."

"I can't. I can see the drop."

Arjuna sighed. "Then the only way is straight up."

"Isn't that dangerous?"

"You won't go forward, you won't go back, neither of us wants to go over the edge. That leaves only up. Think of it like this," he reasoned, "you won't see the drop going up."

We scrambled up the slope in a washed out vertical gully. Hand over hand through the thorn bushes, hugging the earth, grabbing for any hold, we slid back two feet for every five we climbed. A rock flew out beneath me. As I slid, a thorn bush knocked the sunglasses off my face. Arjuna caught them in mid-air, six feet below me. I anchored myself to another rock.

He handed the glasses up. Reaching to grab them, I saw clear down to the river. A company of vultures was feasting on something that had fallen and crashed onto the rocks below. I started scuttling up the crevice like a human spider. My hands and arms were scratched and bleeding. I was running on adrenalin and hysteria, grateful for any purchase, thorns or not. I refused to look back again.

At last we reached a shelf in the cliff face. We were safe. I threw my pack to the ground and burst into tears. They were not tears that required response. I was rocking on my heels, waving my arms and sobbing loudly, without control. Just as suddenly I stopped and sat on my pack. I was somewhat embarrassed.

"You saved my life."

He also looked a little self-conscious.

"Not really. You would have figured it out on your own. I did save your glasses, though." He cocked his head to the side. "I never saw you go so fast. You looked like a river rat running from the flood."

Our laughter was a good release. He brought out the canteen. We shared some water. I touched the dust and thanked the earth for my life. We climbed up a gentler incline and over the lip to another ledge. On the ground, six men were sitting crosslegged in a semi-circle facing us and the river. They exhibited no surprise at our arrival.

One man looked up as we passed, but no one spoke. They reminded me of a company I'd come upon once in Marca Huasi, a fourteen thousand foot plateau jutting up like a tooth from a valley floor in Peru. It was during the festival of Saint Lucas, the patron saint of livestock. The men had been sitting around a gunny sack on the ground, sort of humming. Among the coca leaves on the sacks was the small stone statue of a cow. They also had said nothing.

We walked down the wide corridor of the Kali Gandaki river valley, heading into a wind that steadily increased as the day wore on. It was a phenomenon of air pressure difference between the hot lowlands and the Tibetan plateau that caused the air to come rushing up every afternoon. By the time we reached Jomosom, the first big town on the trek, the wind felt like a constant thirty miles an hour.

We entered a restaurant whose doors closed tightly against the wind and dust. Each table was covered with a thick tablecloth that reached the floor. A heavy set woman padded out and asked indifferently what we wanted to eat.

What do you order from the menu on the day you almost died? In what way do you show your gratitude?

"Beautiful house you have," I said.

The woman smiled and called her daughter, who crawled under our tablecloth, and lit the brazier placed on the floor beneath the table. The girl fanned the coals, and a warmth crept up my legs to the cloth at my lap.

What does one do to celebrate being alive? A roar overhead announced the arrival of a plane. I ordered the specialty of the house, which turned out to be noodles swimming in grease.

Outside, we came upon a dozen Westerners walking in twos and threes. Since we'd passed no one on the road, I assumed they must have arrived by plane. Perhaps the trekking season had already begun. Into the wall of wind Arjuna and I headed down to Marpha, a town of stone walls and cobblestone streets that reminded me of Bagarchap on the Marsyangdi River side.

In the following days the weather got clearer, and we lost elevation steadily. The work for the heart and thighs was replaced by work for the knees. Daulagiri, the 26,000 foot giant to the west, and Nilgiri, 22,000 feet high to the east, stayed with us as we descended. In such illustrious company, it was hard to maintain any sense of self-importance beyond the time it took to look up.

Below Tatopani, we left the Kali Gandaki river valley and began a slow ascent. In a lush rhododendron forest we caught up with three women who looked like the matriarchal line of a family: grandmother, mother, and daughter. Dressed in colorful clothes and wearing dozens of glass bracelets that tinkled as they walked, they said they were bound for a wedding in a nearby town.

After we walked together a while, the old woman turned to Arjuna.

"How poor she must be, and how poor her husband!" She began to laugh. "Here our husbands give us gold."

She was pointing to the red string on my marriage finger. I had found a strand of new red yarn on the path that morning, and wound it onto my conglomerate of string, making it thicker and brighter. She had a well worn marriage band, as did her daughter. The granddaughter, a beautiful woman of about fifteen, would soon wear a gold band of her own, I thought.

I laughed with them. "Yes, yes. No money, my husband."

The old woman looked shrewdly at Arjuna. "You are not her husband."

Arjuna grinned. "No, I am not."

"She should look for another one."

The dialogue started to assume a larger meaning. The kindness

I was trying to practice toward myself and others—was I married to the concept of honoring the spirit in that way? Yes, I was. Just as in the practice of bowing *Namaste,* wearing the red string reminded me of the spirit—goddess or god—in everything, even in my thoughts.

I shook my head. "No, no other. Beautiful, my husband."

The old woman went into gales of laughter. Her breasts shook. A gold tooth in the back of her mouth came into view. When we got to a waterfall, she stopped to catch her breath. Her daughter and granddaughter sat beside her. We could still hear her chirping merrily behind us as we hurried on.

After climbing steadily all day, we reached GhoDapani and took the side road up to Poon Hill. From its vantage point, sticking up from the valley floor, Poon Hill had an unparalleled view of the mountains, starting with Dhaulagiri in the north, and stretching all the way around to Machhapuchhare in the east.

In the inn near the top, the enterprising innkeeper had rigged up outdoor hot showers with wooden floors, and clean toilets with ample water to flush. In the main room was a large fire pit and chimney for warmth at night. On the menu were several kinds of cooked greens for dinner, and apple pancakes for dessert. We had lucked into an outpost of luxury I'd forgotten existed.

At twilight a young Belgian couple arrived, bound for the Thorung La. They were both painters. Besides their sleeping bags and personal things, they carried easels, paints, paper, and a waterproof portfolio. In the firelight after dinner, they rolled out their paintings.

The woman had a series of black and white abstracts that looked like mountains. The man had just finished a watercolor landscape of mountains, rolling hills, and valleys. On closer inspection, it was also a woman covered in earth-colored bits of cloth, sleeping on the ground like the beggars of Kathmandu. The couple intended to paint and sketch their way across the Himalayas. Their enthusiasm was contagious.

The next morning I rose before dawn and climbed above the inn for the sunrise. With a compass and map I identified the great Dhaulagiri, Tukuche Peak, Nilgiri from the south, Baraha Shikhar, Annapurna Dakshin that I'd been seeing for the last two days, Hiunchuli, and just the tip of Machhapuchhare, the fish-tailed mountain. There they were.

In the silence the sun spread across the peaks and filled in the nooks and crannies of each glacier against the sky, and the razor back ridgelines that rose and fell below. In the face of such beauty, I had no questions. I belonged to that landscape. Like the sleeping woman in the painting, I was part of those mountains and they were part of me.

From Poon Hill, Ullieri was a four thousand foot descent for the knees. The population of hikers on the trail steadily increased. Inside the town we came upon a bustling congress of sixty British librarians having tea on the terrace of a cafe, overlooking the spectacular view. They seemed to make it official: tourist season had started.

The way down from Ullieri was an amazing engineering feat of thousands of stone steps down to the valley floor. All the grains we'd passed on the ascent—rice, millet, buckwheat, barley, wheat—were being harvested. The waves of grain had turned into food. When we stopped to eat, our innkeeper was drying millet on the terrace—to make his beer, he said. In the field above us, the unharvested black seed pods bent toward each other like fingers.

Instead of resting after lunch, I felt an urgency to push on. Arjuna suggested that since we were just two days from Pokhara, the end of the trek, we could afford to relax. But he joined me nonetheless, and we kept up a good trotting pace down the long stairs. I couldn't say why I was hurrying, only that I was anxious to keep going.

In Hille we agreed to stop for a drink. Arjuna pointed to a restaurant, but I shook my head. I was looking for something else. On the far side of town was the last place, a hotel with a patio cafe.

I plunged in, headed for one of the empty tables, and rested my pack against the chair. When the boy came to take our order, I asked for two sodas.

As he turned to go, I understood what had driven me. Across the patio was the Danish woman who had fallen in the stream. Erica. She jumped up when she saw us, and called to her husband in one of the rooms. We were all grinning as they sat down. Her scar was a crudely sewn black cuneiform wedge, but it was closed and healed, and she was healthy.

They had just started out two days before from Pokhara, and were on their way up to Muktinath. The hospital in Kathmandu had said her stitches, although primitive, were fine. She and Niels had waited until she was completely healed before heading out again. The fall had made them philosophical. If they made it as far as the pass, fine; if not, that was fine, too. When the boy brought the sodas, we toasted the road that had brought us together twice. After a time Arjuna stood up. If we left immediately we could make it to the next town by dark.

In Berethanti, the growing trekker population crowded the inns; but I felt my distance from the Nepalis increase, and our interchange was becoming minimal. The hikers' attitude toward Arjuna as a porter made my hackles rise. I was quick to point out that we had both made it over the pass, thanks to him, but their ignorance would not be enlightened by my anger. I rubbed the string on my finger and left the dining room.

At dawn I was awakened by a loud complaint. A water buffalo, whose stall was directly across from my window, brayed like a baritone sax as he called for breakfast. On the road again with Arjuna, I was conscious that it was our last day walking. The sun shone on the grain in the fields, ripe for harvest, and I felt already homesick for the lands I had covered, nostalgic over the wheat I had watched growing.

We heard children's voices down by the river. As we rounded the bend, two little girls came into view, heading up the bank. They were about six years old. Their arms were filled with wild flowers—red, yellow, pink, orange, purple—in all shapes and sizes. The girls did not see us. They were singing together as they walked along. In the face of such sweetness, it was hard to stayed fixed on loss.

As we made our way down toward civilization, the heat increased. The landscape became boring in the sense that it was not itself. The earth had been gouged out and moved to make way for a greatly enlarged highway. Flimsy shacks had crept in to house the workers or the equipment, and the litter of trekkers increased alarmingly. Men shouted over the roar of machines. We hitched a ride along the new stretch of road in the truck of Chinese engineers.

The center of Pokhara was a bustling tourist mecca, where the dusty streets were lined with stalls of merchandise, and no one looked anyone else in the eye. No nods, no smiles, no *Namastes*. We ate a great meal in a fancy restaurant, and I booked us passage on the next bus to Kathmandu. I wrote in my journal:

> At the end of the road
> there is no fair haven
> no hero's welcome
> no pot of tea
> at the end of the road
> is the road
>
> stretching in both directions
> in your heart.

It was October in the marketplace of Kathmandu. The daily downpour I remembered was replaced by clouds of dust. Kamala, a beautiful Nepali woman who ran a yogurt stand, told me people were preparing for Dewali, the festival of lights, and the Hindu new year. It was the time to honor Lakshmi, the goddess of wealth, beauty, and plenty.

She showed me a picture. Lakshmi was standing on a lotus in the water. She had a book in one hand, a flower in another; the third held what looked like the energy of creation; the fourth hand poured down gold coins like a blessing. It was the goddess I'd seen in the courtyard when the old man had shown me how to worship, my first week in Kathmandu. With the fields I'd passed ready for harvest, and the trees ripe with fruit, I could understand why the season belonged to Lakshmi.

My flight to Amsterdam was confirmed; I would leave in four days. I had not forgotten my original quest: to find the Mother underneath the male layers. The female divinity. And I wanted to salute the one I'd dreamt of, up by the Thorung La. It seemed to me that by entering Pasupatinath and honoring the presence there I would be completing a circle.

I canvased everyone I knew. Could anyone get me in? One person knew the cousin of the gatekeeper, another the ex-wife of the king's brother. A third counseled me to dress like a Western devotee of a certain sadu he knew. Everyone promised to help. Meanwhile, I rattled through the Thamel with the throngs of tourists arriving daily.

Time passed and nothing happened, until one morning I stepped into the rug bazaar across from the hotel. The men whose shop it was were all part of one family, and the closest thing I had to neighbors. Their sons had taught me how to count when I'd arrived. The middle brother waved me to a stool and asked why I looked unhappy. I explained my need to enter the temple, then thought to ask for their help.

To my surprise, all three brothers were outraged. Shiva was male, they said. He was male, there was no question about that. The face? The body? Absolutely male. Pasupatinath was sacred to Hindus. Under no circumstances should a Westerner, and female at that, be allowed inside.

I countered that I was a poet; and poets belonged to all religions. Didn't they see I wanted to enter the temple in respect? And others here had promised to help me.

"No, no!" the eldest brother shouted. "Anything but that! This is the king's religion—you cannot enter!"

I strode from the store before my anger got away from me, and stopped at the corner. The old man who usually sat on a box outside the religious artifacts store was at his post. He was soaking up the sun, as he often did, talking with the shop owner. Behind him were Buddhas, thunderbolts, incense trays, prayer wheels, Tibetan drums—every artifact one might need to practice Buddhism, shamanism, or Hinduism. The old man twirled a prayer wheel unobtrusively in his right hand, by his knee. Engaged in conversation, he was also praying.

Why was I angry? Coming to Nepal and walking over the Annapurnas, I had also been doing something else. I had been asking for something. And hadn't I found that the Shakti they spoke of was everything in creation? She was the mountains and the devotion of the people and their kindness to a stranger, who was also Her. She was the flow of thought and the words one used to describe her bounty. She was the energy breaking through for necessary change. I had no need to go hammering on the doors of any temple, where she might be celebrated but more than likely wasn't. I had only to wait. Whatever happened was what should happen. The civil engineer in Bagarchap would have agreed.

In a cafe I met my friend Dominique, the woman who had gone with me to Pasupatinath. She had a sore on her leg that was seriously infected. She'd spent most of the time that I'd been gone taking antibiotics, sitting in the cafes, and waiting for her leg to heal.

I asked if she were strong enough to go shopping, and she jumped up, welcoming the diversion. I needed gifts for home. We walked through the dusty market, into store after store. When she entered a shop I'd already been to, I headed for the puppet store across the way.

The puppets were not toys. They represented different aspects of goddesses and gods, and had either two faces, front and back—with accompanying hands and feet—or four. It was difficult to discern which deities they were, so I chose on the basis of color. I was partial to red.

The owner was a short, good-looking man in his thirties, with thick black hair. He came over to where I stood. Looking at the two-sided puppet in my hand, he spoke as though resuming a conversation.

"The presence of the female is just as strong as the male—perhaps stronger—though you might not guess it from what you see around you."

He gestured toward the street, and the woman walking several steps behind her husband. Holding on to one end of her sari, she was not hurrying to come alongside him, but seemed deliberately to stay behind.

"But that is not it," he concluded.

A motorcycle passed. The man studied the dust as it settled to the ground.

"No matter what the appearance, it is not male, it is not female." He was enunciating his words as though I had trouble understanding English. "It is fire. You can't touch the fire. The fire is stone. You can't touch the stone. And that's it. That is what we worship. That is what is in the temple. That's it."

The hair on my arms was standing up; the top of my scalp was tingling. I turned to say something, but he had hurried away. A German couple was standing on the street with their arms full of puppets they wanted to buy.

Anyway, what would I say? I felt like I'd been included in something and could no longer ask what face it wore or what I should do. I went to pay for the puppets and the man looked at me.

"So that's it? That's all you need?"

I nodded. He might have meant my purchase but I didn't think so. I took the change and bowed *Namaste.*

The following morning, I was packed and ready. I had just enough time to go down to Pasupatinath. I took a cab. Getting out in the heat, I made a slow circle around the great walls, across the river, and back again. I circled Durga in her temple of blood. I bowed every place I stopped, and did not try at any of the gates to gain entry. Then I headed back up through the market.

A woman selling glass bangles called me. She motioned for me to sit before her on the ground. She pointed to the different colored glass bracelets, but I shook my head. I pointed to my hands, which are very large, and the bangles, which looked so small. I indicated they would never fit.

The woman looked behind her at another woman, also seated on the ground with her wares around her. My woman had me hold out my hand. One by one, she slipped the delicate glass bracelets over the thumb joint and onto my wrist. Nine red bracelets. I was delighted. They would never come off again, I thought, unless they broke.

I took out money to pay her, but she shook her head. They were a gift. I loved the way they looked, and the way they tinkled. They reminded me of the woman I'd seen outside Pasupatinath the first time, stretching luxuriously over her oranges in the shady courtyard. And they made me feel the same way—like a priestess or a prostitute, whose first site of pilgrimage was the body, and whose secret office resided in the temple she carried around.

It suddenly occurred to me to buy more. I could replace them if any broke, or give them away. My friends would love them. I picked out a dozen bracelets, and the woman looked over at her friend again, as though they knew something I did not. She held out her open palm for payment.

I counted out the money. Then I slipped another bracelet over my wrist as she had done. It snapped in two pieces. Both women burst out laughing. I tried another, it also broke. It seemed what she had given me I could not give myself. I dropped the purchase into my pocket, and bowed *Namaste*. My bracelets jingled as I hurried for a cab.

In my room I showered, dressed, and was ready to go. Friends from the Thamel came by to see me off. They were helping me zip up the bags when Arjuna came in.

"So you're ready to go?"

I nodded and smiled. Despite our respectively stubborn natures, he'd become a good friend.

"I have something for you," he said. Out of a paper bag he took a plastic envelope of red powder. He dipped his finger into it, and touched my forehead between the eyes. *Tika.* He sprinkled the rest of the powder on his fingers over my shoulders. Then he pulled out a garland of bright yellow marigolds and placed it around my neck.

I tried not to show how touched I was.

"I can't get on a plane with this thing. I look like I'm going to a luau."

Everyone laughed. But the fact was, when I touched the flowers and my bracelets jingled, I felt like those women at the waterfall. I felt like I was dressed for a wedding.

Recommended Reading

Bezruchka, Stephen. *A Guide to Trekking in Nepal*. Seattle, Wa.: The Mountaineers, 1985.

Dames, Michael. *The Silbury Treasure: The Great Goddess Rediscovered*. London: Thames & Hudson, 1976.

Danielou, Alain. *The Myths and Gods of India*. Rochester, Vt: Inner Traditions International, 1991.

David-Neel, Alexandra. *Magic and Mystery in Tibet*. Baltimore, MD: Penguin Books, 1929.

Fortune, Dion. *Avalon of the Heart*. N.Y.: Samuel Weiser, 1971.

Gimbutas, Marija. *The Language of the Goddess*. NY: HarperCollins, 1989.

Hoult, Janet. *A Short History of the Dragon*. Glastonbury, Eng.: Gothic Image, 1978.

Jagadiswarananda, Swami, tr. *Devi Mahatmyam; Glory of the Divine Mother: 700 Mantras on Sri Durga*. Madras, India: Sri Ramakrishna Math, 1953.

Maltwood, K.E. *A Guide to Glastonbury's Temple of the Stars: Their Giant Effigies Described from Air Views, Maps, and from "The High History of the Holy Grail."* London: James Clarke & Co. Ltd.: 1964.

Mattiessen, Peter and Thomas Laird. *East of Lo Monthang*. Boston, Ma.: Shamballa, 1995.

Merton, Thomas. *Ishi Means Man*. Greensboro, N.C.: Unicorn Press, 1976.

Pinkola Estes, Clarissa. *Women Who Run with the Wolves*. NY: Ballantine Books, 1992.

Rufus, Anneli S. & Lawson, Kristan. *Goddess Sites: Europe: Places Where the Goddess Has Been Celebrated and Worshiped Throughout Time*. San Francisco, Ca.: Harper San Francisco, 1990.

Shaw, Miranda. *Passionate Enlightenment; Women in Tantric Buddhism in India*. Princeton, NJ: Princeton University Press, 1994.

Yeats, William Butler. *Stories of Red Hanrahan: Mythologies*. London: Macmillan & Co. Ltd., 1959.